Two Lamentable Tragedies

The Tudor Facsimile Texts

Two Lamentable Tragedies

by ROBERT YARRINGTON.

Date of only known quarto 1601

Reproduced in Facsimile 1913

The Tudor Facsimile Texts

Under the Supervision and Editorship of

JOHN S. FARMER

Two Lamentable Tragedies

by ROBERT YARRINGTON.

1601

Issued for Subscribers by the Editor of

THE TUDOR FACSIMILE TEXTS

MCMXIII

𝔗𝔴𝔬 𝔏𝔞𝔪𝔢𝔫𝔱𝔞𝔟𝔩𝔢 𝔗𝔯𝔞𝔤𝔢𝔡𝔦𝔢𝔰

BY ROB. YARRINGTON.

1601

This reproduction of the only known edition is from the British Museum copy. Bodley has a copy and two or three others are known.

"The Dictionary of National Biography," speaking of this play and its author, says. " Nothing has been discovered concerning Robert Yarrington In 'Henslowe's Diary' (ed. Collier, pp 92-3) we find that in 1599 Haughton & Day wrote a tragedy called 'The tragedy of Thomas Merrye.' This was clearly on the first subject of Yarrington's play. The next entry in the 'Diary' refers to 'The Orphanes Tragedy' by Chettle, which was apparently never finished. This would seem to be the second subject of Yarrington's play. Mr. Fleay conjectures that Rob. Yarrington is a fictitious name, and that his play is an amalgamation of the two plays by Haughton, Day & Chettle. Mr. A. H. Bullen republished the play with an introduction in a collection of 'Old English Plays' 1885, vol. IV."

The reproduction of this facsimile is satisfactory ; the original is more or less stained and the paper in places worn into holes which are readily noticed in this facsimile.

JOHN S. FARMER.

Two Lamentable Tragedies,

The one, of the murther of Mai-
ster Beech *a Chaundler in*
Thames-streete, and his boye,
done by *Thomas Merry*.

The other of a young childe mur-
thered in a Wood by two Ruffins,
with the consent of his Vnckle.

By Rob. Yarington,

London
Printed for *Mathew Lawe*, and are to be solde at
his shop in Paules Church-yarde neere vnto
S. Austines gate, at the signe
of the Foxe. 1601.

Two Tragedies
in one.

Enter Homicide, *solus.*

I Haue in vaine paſt through each ſtately
    ſtreete,
And blinde-fold turning of this happie
    towne,
For wealth , for peace , and goodlie
    gouernement,
      Yet can I not finde out a minde, a heart
For blood and cauſeleſſe death to harbour in;
They all are bent with vertuous gainefull trade,
To get their needmentes for this mortall life,
And will not ſoile their well addicted harts:
With rape, extortion, murther, or the death,
Of friend or foe, to gaine an Empery.
I cannot glut my blood delighted eye;
With mangled bodies which do gaſpe and grone,
Readie to paſſe to faire *Elizium,*
Nor bath my greedie handes in reeking blood,
Of fathers by their children murthered:
When all men elſe do weepe, lament and waile,
The ſad exploites of fearefull tragedies,
It glads me ſo, that it delightes my heart,
To ad new tormentes to their bleeding ſmartes.
        Enter Auarice.
But here comes *Auarice,* as if he ſought,
Some buſie worke for his pernicious thought:

                Whe-

Whether so fast all griping *Auarice?*

Aua. Why what earst thou, I seeeke for one I misse.

Ho. I may supplie the man you wish to haue,

Aua. Thou seemes to be a bold audatious knaue,
I doe not like intruding companie,
That seeke to vndermine my secrecie.

Ho. Mistrust me not I am thy faithfull friend.

Aua. Many say so, that proue false in the end.

Ho. But turne about and thou wilt know my face,

Aua. It may be so, and know thy want of grace,
What *Homicide* thou art the man I seeke:
I reconcile me thus vpon thy cheeke.   *Kisse, imbrace.*
Hadst thou nam'd blood and damn'd iniquitie,
I had for borne to bight so bitterlie.

Hom. Knowst thou a hart wide open to receiue,
A plot of horred desolation,
Tell me of this, thou art my cheefest good,
And I will quaffe thy health in bowles of blood.

Aua. I know two men, that seeme two innocents,
Whose lookes surueied with iudiciall eyes:
Would seeme to beare the markes of honestie,
But snakes finde harbour mongst the fairest flowers,
Then neuer credit outward semblaunces:

                    Enter Truth.
I know their harts relentlesse mercilesse,
And will performe through hope of benefit:
More dreadfull things then can be thought vpon.

Hom. If gaine will draw, I prethy then allure,
Their hungrie harts with hope of recompence,
But tye dispaire vnto those moouing hopes,
Vnleast a deed of murther farther it,
Then blood on blood, shall ouertake them all,
And we will make a bloodie feastiuall.

Coue. The plots are laide, the keyes of golden coine,
Hath op'd the secret closets of their harts,
Inter, insult, make captiue at thy will,

                                        Them-

Themselues,and friends,with deedes of damned ill;
Yonder is truth,she commeth to bewaile,
The times and parties that we worke vpon.

Hom. Why let her weepe,lament,and morne for me,
We are right bred of damn'd iniquitie,
And will go make a two-solde Tragedie.   *Exeunt.*

Truth. Goe you disturbers of a quiet soule,
Sad, greedy,gaping,hungrie *Canibals;*
That ioy to practise others miseries;
Gentles,prepare your teare bedecked eyes,
To see two shewes of lamentation,
Besprinckled euery where with guiltlesse blood,
Of harmlesse youth,and pretie innocents,
Our Stage doth weare habilliments of woe,
Truth rues to tell the truth of these laments;
The one was done in famous London late,
Within that streete whose side the riuer Thames
Doth striue to wash from all impurities:
But yet that siluer streame can neuer wash,
The sad remembrance of that cursed deede,
Perform'd by cruell *Merry* on iust *Beech,*
And his true boye poore *Thomas Winchester,*
The most here present,know this to be true;
Would truth were false,so this were but a tale,
The other further off,but yet too neere,
To those that felt and did the crueltie:
Neere *Padua* this wicked deed was done,
By a false Vncle, on his brothers sonne,
Left to his carefull education,
By dying Parents,with as strict a charge,
As euer yet death-breathing brother gaue:
Looke for no mirth,vnlesse you take delight,
In mangled bodies,and in gaping wounds,
Bloodily made by mercy wanting hands,
Truth will not faine,but yet doth grieue to showe,
This deed of ruthe and miserable woe,

Enter

Enter Merry.

I liue in meane and difcontented ftate,
But wherefore fhould I thinke of difcontent:
I am belou'd, I haue a pretty houfe,
A louing fifter, and a carefull man,
That doe not thinke their dayes worke well at end,
Except it bring me in fome benefit:
And well frequented is my little houfe,
With many gueftes and honeft paffengers,

Enter Beech *and a friend.*

Which may in time aduance my humble ftate;
To greater wealth and reputation.
And here comes friends to drinke fome beare or ale, *Sit in*
They are my neighbours, they fhall haue the beft, *his fhop.*
Ne. Come neighbor *Beech* lets haue our mornings draught
And wele go drinke it at yong *Merries* houfe:
They fay he hath the beft in all this towne,
Befides they fay he is an honeft man,
And keepes good rule and orders in his houfe.
  Beech. He's fo indeede, his conuerfation,
Is full of honeft harmleffe curtefie:
I dare prefume, if that he be within,
Hele ferue vs well, and keepe vs company,
See where he is, go in, ile follow you.   *Striue curtefie.*
Nay ftraine no curtefie you fhall goe before.
  Mer. Your welcome neighbour, you are welcome fir,
I praie fit downe, your verie welcome both:
  Beech. We thanke you for it, and we thinke no leffe,
Now fill two cans of your ould ftrongeft beare:
That make fo manie loofe their little wits,
And make indentures as they go along.
  Mer. Hoe fifter *Rachell*:   *Rach.* I come prefently.

Enter Rachell.

  Mer. Goe draw thefe gentlemen two Cans of beare,
Your negligence that cannot tend the fhop,
Willl make our cuftomers forfake the houfe.
Wheres *Harry Williams* that he ftaies not here.
                                              Rach.

Rach. My selfe was busie dressing vp the house,
As for your man he is not verie well:
But sitteth sleeping by the kitchen fier.

Mer. If you are busie get you vp againe,　　　　*Exit.*
Ile draw my neighbours then their drinke my selfe,
Ile warrant you as good as any mans,
And yet no better, many haue the like.　　*Exit for Beare.*

Neigh. This showes him for a plaine and honest man,
That will not flatter with too many wordes:
Some shriltong'd fellowes would haue cogd and faind,
Saying ile draw the best in Christendome.

Beech. Hees none of those, but beares an honest minde,
And shames to vtter what he cannot proue.

　　　　　　Enter Merry.

But here he comes, is that the best you haue,

Mer. It is the best vpon mine honest worde.

Beech. Then drinke to vs.　*Mer.* I drinke vnto you both.

Nei. Beech. We pledge you both, and thanke you hartelie.

Beech. Heres to you sir. *Neigh.* I thanke you,
　　　　　Maister Beech *drinkes, drinke* Neighbour.

Neigh. Tis good indeed and I had rather drinke,
Such beare as this as any Gascoine wine:
But tis our English manner to affect
Strange things, and price them at a greater rate,
Then home-bred things of better consequence.

Mer. Tis true indeede, if all were of your minde,
My poore estate would sooner be aduanc'd:
And our French Marchants seeke some other trade.

Beech. Your poore estate, nay neighbour say not so,
For God be thanked you are well to liue.

Mer. Not so good neighbour, but a poore young man,
That would liue better if I had the meanes:
But as I am, I can content my selfe,
Till God amend my poore abilitie.

Neigh. In time no doubt, why man you are but young,
And God assure your selfe hath wealth in store,
If you awaight his will with patience.

　　　　　　A 4　　　　　　　　　*Beech.*

Two Tragedies in one.

Beech. Thankes be to God I liue contentedlie,
And yet I cannot boast of mightie wealth:
But yet Gods blessings haue beene infinit,
And farre beyond my expectations,
My shop is stor'd, I am not much in debt:
And here I speake it where I may be bold,
I haue a score of poundes to helpe my neede,
If God should stretch his hand to visit me,
With sicknesse, or such like aduersity.

Neigh. Enough for this, now neighbour whats to pay,
Mer. Two pence good sir. *Beech.* Nay pray sir forbeare,
Ile pay this reckoning for it is but small.

Neigh. I will not striue since yee will haue it so.
Beech. Neighbour fare well.   *Exit Beech and neigh.*
Mer. Farewell vnto you both.
His shop is stor'd he is not much indebt,
He hath a score of poundes to helpe his neede,
I and a score too if the trueth were knowne:
I would I had a shop so stor'd with wares,
And fortie poundes to buy a bargaine with,
When as occasion should be offered me,
Ide liue as merrie as the wealthiest man,
That hath his being within London walles,
I cannot buy my beare, my bread, my meate:
My fagots, coales, and such like necessaries,
At the best hand, because I want the coine,
That manie misers coafer vp in bagges,
Hauing enough to serue their turnes besides:
Ah for a tricke to make this *Beeches* trash,
Forsake his cofer and to rest in mine,
I marrie sir, how may that tricke be done:
Marrie with ease and great facilitie,
I will inuent some new-found stratagem,
To bring his coyne to my possession,
What though his death relieue my pouertie,
Gaine waites on courage, losse on cowardice.

                                            Enter

Two Tragedies in one.

Enter Pandino and Armenia sicke on a bed, Pertillo their soune, Falleria his brother, Sostrato his wife, Alinso their sonne, and a Scriuener with a VVill, &c.

Pan. Brother and sister, pray you both drawe neere,
And heere my will, which you haue promised
Shall be performde with wished prouidence,
This little Orphant I mu ft leaue behinde,
By your direction to be gouerned.
As for my wife and I, we do awaite,
The blessed houre when it shall please the Lord,
To take vs to the iust Ierusalem.
Our chiefest care is for that tender boye,
Which we should leaue discomfortlesse behinde,
But that we do assure vs of your loue,
And care to guide his weake vnhable youth,
In pathes of knowledge grace and godlinesse:
As for the riches of this mortall life,
We leaue enough, foure hundreth pounds a yeare,
Besides two thousand pounds to make a stocke,
In money, Iewels, Plate, and houshold stuffe,
Which yearely rents and goods we leaue to you,
To be surrendered into his hands,
When he attaines to yeeres of discreation.
My Will imports thus much, which you shall heare,
And you shall be my sole Executor.

Fall: Brother and sister how my hart laments,
To see your weake and sicke afflicted limmes,
Neere ouercome with dyrefull malladies,
The God of heauen can truely testifie,
Which to speake plaine, is nere a whit at all. *To the people,*
Which knowes the secret corners of my heart,
But for the care you do impose on me,
For the tuition of your little sonne,
Thinke my kinde brother, I will meditate,
Both day and night, how I may best fulfill,

B   The

The care and truſt, repoſed in your Will,
And ſee him poſted quickly after you.   *To the people.*

  Arm. Enough kinde brother, we aſſure vs ſo,
Elſe would we ſeeke another friend abroade,
To do our willes and dying Teſtament,
Nature and loue will haue a double care,
To bring him vp with carefull dilligence,
As beſt beſeemes one of ſuch parentage.

  Fall. Aſſure your ſelfe the ſafeſt courſe I can,
Shall be prouided for your little ſonne,
He ſhall be ſent vnto the King of heauen.   *To the people.*

  Soſtr. Feare not good brother, and my louing ſiſter,
But we will haue as tender care of him,
As if he were our owne ten thouſand times:
God will be father of the fatherleſſe,
And keepe him from all care and wretchedneſſe.

  Allenſo. Vnckle and Aunt take comfort, I will ſee,
My little coozen haue no iniurie.

  Pan. Ar. We thanke you all, come let the Will be read.
  Fall. If it were ſeald, I would you both were dead.
  Scrine. Then giue attention, I will read the Will.

     Reade the VVill.

In the name of God, e Amen . I, &c.

  Pan. Thus if my ſonne miſcarry, my deare brother,
You and your ſonne ſhall then enioy the land,
And all the goods which he ſhould haue poſſeſſd,

  Fall. If he miſcarry, brother God forbid,
God bleſſe mine Nephew, that thine eyes may ſee,
Thy childrens children with proſperity :
I had rather ſee the little vrchin hangd,   *To the people.*
Then he ſhould liue, and I forgoe the land.

  Ar. Thankes gentle brother, husband ſeale the Will.

  Pand. Giue me a Pen and Inke, firſt to ſubſcribe,
I write ſo ill through very feebleneſſe,
That I can ſcarcely know this hand for mine,
But that you all can witneſſe that it is.

  Seri. Giue me the ſeale ; I pray ſir take it of,

                            This

This you deliuer for your latest Will,
And do confirme it for your Testament.

    Pend. With all my hart : here brother keepe my Will,
And I referre me to the will of God,
Praying him deale aswell with you and yours,
As you no doubt will deale with my poore child:
Come my *Pertillo,*let me blesse thee boy,
And lay my halfe dead hand vpon thy head,
God graunt those dayes that are cut off in me,
With ioy and peace may multiply in thee:
Be flowe to wrath, obey thy Vnckle still,
Submit thy selfe vnto Gods holy will,
In deede and word, see thou be euer true,
So brother, childe, and kinssolkes all adue.   *He dyeth.*

    Per. Ah my deere mother, is my father dead ?
    Ar. I my sweete Boye, his soule to heauen is fled,
But I shall after him immediatly,
Then take my latest blessing ere I dye,
Come let me kisse thy little tender lips,
Cold death hath tane possession of thy mother.
Let me imbrace thee in my dying armes,
And pray the lord protect thee from al harmes:
Brother, I feare, this childe when I am gone,
Wil haue great cause of griese & hideous feare:
You will protect him, but I prophecie,
His share will be of woe and misery :
But mothers feares do make these cares arise,
Come boye and close thy mothers dying eyes.
Brother and sister, here the latest words,
That your dead sister leaues for memory :
If you deale ill with this distressed boye,
God will reuenge poore orphants iniuries,
If you deale well, as I do hope you will,
God will defend both you and yours from ill.
Farewell, farewell, now let me breath my last,
Into his dearest mouth, that wanteth breath,
And as we lou'd in life imbrace in death ;

                               Bro.

Brother and sister this is all I pray,
Tender my Boye when we are laide in clay. *Dyeth.*

Allen. Gods holy Angell guide your louing soules,
Vnto a place of endlesse happinesse.

Softr. Amen, Amen, ah what a care she had,
Of her small Orphant, she did dying pray,
To loue her childe, when she was laide in claye.

Scr. Ah blame her not although she held it deare,
She left him yonge the greater cause of feare.

Fall. Knew she my minde, it would recall her life, *To*
And like a staring Commet she would mooue, *the people.*
Our harts to thinke of desolation,
Scriuenor, haue you certified the will?

Scri. I haue.

Fall. Then theres two Duckets for your paines.

Scri. Thankes gentle sir, and for this time farewell. *Exit.*

Soft. Come prety coozen, cozened by grim death,
Of thy most carefull parents all too-soone,
Weepe not sweete boy, thou shalt haue cause to say,
Thy Aunt was kinde, though parents lye in claye.

Pert. But giue me leaue first to lament the losse,
Of my deere Parents, nature bindeth me,
To waile the death of those that gaue me life,
And if I liue vntill I be a man,
I will erect a sumptuous monument,
And leaue remembrance to ensuing times,
Of kinde *Pandino* and *Armenia.*

Allen. That shall not neede, my father will erect,
That sad memoriall of their timeles death,
And at that tombe we will lament and say
Soft lye the bones of faire *Armenia.*

Fall. Surcease *Allenso*, thats a bootelesse cost,
The Will imports no such iniunction:
I will not spend my little Nephewes wealth,
In such vaine toyes, they shall haue funerall,
But with no stately ceremoniall pompe,
Thats good for nought but fooles to gase vppon,

Liue

Liue thou in hope to haue thine vnckles land.

Aller. His land, why father you haue land enough,
And more by much then I do know to vſe:
I would his vertues would in me ſuruiue,
So ſhould my Vnckle ſeeme in me aliue,
But to your will I doe ſubmit my ſelfe,
Do what you pleaſe concerning funeralls.

Fal. Come then away, that we may take in hand,
To haue poſſeſſion of my brothers land,
His goods and all vntill he come of age:
To rule and gouerne ſuch poſſeſſions.
That ſhalbe neuer or ile miſſe my marke,
Till I ſurrender vp my life to death:
And then my ſonne ſhalbe his fathers heire,
And mount aloft to honors happy chaire.

Exeunt : Omnes.

Enter Merry *ſolus.*

Beech hath a ſcore of pounds to helpe his neede,
And I may ſtarue ere he will lend it me:
But in diſpight ile haue it ere I ſleepe,
Although I ſend him to eternall reſt,
But ſhallow foole, thou talkſt of mighty things,
And canſt not compaſſe what thou doſt conceiue:
Stay let me ſee, ile fetch him to my houſe,
And in my garret quickly murther him :
The night conceales all in her pitchie cloake,
And none can open what I meane to hide,
But then his boy will ſay I fetcht him foorth :
I am reſolu'd, he ſhall be murthered to,
This toole ſhall write, ſubſcribe, and ſeale their death,
And ſend them ſafely to anotl er world :
But then my ſiſter, and my man at home,
Will not conceale it when the deede is done,
Tuſh one for loue, the other for reward,
Wil' neuer tell the world my cloſe intent,
My conſcience ſaith it is a damned deede:
To traine one foorth, and ſlay him priuily,

B 3

Peace

Peace conscience, peace. thou art too scripulous,
Gaine doth attended this resolution,
Hence dastard feare, I must, I can, I will,
Kill my best friend to get a bag of gold:
They shall dye both, had they a thousand liues,
And therefore I will place this hammer here,
And take it as I follow *Beech* vp staires,
That suddenlie before he is aware;
I may with blowes dash out his hatefull braines,
Hoe *Rachell*, bring my cloake, looke to the house,
I will returne againe immediatly.

Rach. Here it is brother, I pray you stay not long,
Guesse will come in, 'tis almost supper time.   *Ex. Ra.*

Mer. Let others suppe, ile make a bloudier feast,
Then euer yet was drest in *Merryes* house,
Be like thy selfe, then haue a merrie hart,
Thou shalt haue gold to mend thy pouertie,
And after this, liue euer wealthilie.

>   *Then* Merry *must passe to* Beeches *sheppe, who*
>   *must sit in his shop, and* Winchester *his*
>   *boy stand by:* Beech *reading.*

What neighbour *Beech*, so godly occupied?

Beech. I maister *Merry* it were better reade,
Then meditate on idle fantasies.

Mer. You speake the trueth: there is a friend or two
Of yours, making merry in my house,
And would desire to haue your company.

Beech. Know you their names?

Mer. No truely nor the men.
I neuer stoode to question them of that,
But they desire your presence earnestlie.

Beech. I pray you tell them that I cannot come,
Tis supper time, and many will resort,
For ware at this time, aboue all other times;
Tis Friday night besides, and Bartholmew eue,
Therefore good neighbour make my iust excuse.

Mer. In trueth they told me that you should not stay,
                                                    Goe

Goe but to drinke, you may come quick againe,
But not and if my hand and hammer hold.   *Peopls.*

  Beech. I am vnwilling, but I do not care,
And if I go to see the company.

  Mer. Come quickly then, they thinke we stay too long,
  Beich. Ile cut a peece of Cheese to drinke withall.

  Mer. I take the farewell of your cutting knife,
Here is a hand shall helpe to cut your throate:
And giue my selfe a fairing from your chest:
What are you ready will you goe along?

  Beech. I now I am, boy looke you tend the shoppe,
If any aske, come for me to the Bull,
I wonder who they are that aske for me.

  Mer. I know not that, you shall see presentlie,
Goe vp those staires, your friends do stay aboue,
Here is that friend shall shake you by the head,
And make you stagger ere he speake to you.

          Then being in the vpper Rome Merry *strickes*
              him in the head fifteene times.

Now you are safe, I would the boy were so,
But wherefore wish I, for he shall not liue,
For if he doe, I shall not liue my selfe.

          Merry *wiped his face from blood.*

Lets see what mony he hath in his purse,
Masse heres ten groates, heres something for my paine,
But I must be rewarded better yet.

          Enter Rachell *and* Harry Williams.

  Wil. Who was it *Rachell* that went vp the staires?
  Rach. It was my brother, and a little man
Of black complexion, but I know him not,
  Wil. Why do you not then carry vp a light,
But suffer them to tarry in the darke.
  Rach. I had forgot, but I will beare one vp.   *Exit vp.*
  Wil. Do so I prethee, he will chide anon.   *Exit.*

          Rachell *speaketh to her brother.*

  Rachell. Oh brother, brother, what haue you done?
  Mer. Why murtherd one that would haue murtherd me,
                                            Rach.

Beech. We are vndone, brother we are vndone,
What shall I say for we are quite vndone.

Mer. Quiet thy selfe sister, all shalbe well,
But see in any case you do not tell,
This deede to *William:* nor to any one:

Rach. No, no, I will not, was't not maister *Beech?*

Mer. It was, it is, and I will kill his man,   *Exit Rach.*
Or in attempting doe the best I can.

             Enter Williams *and* Rachell.

Wil. What was the matter that you cride so lowde?

Rach. I must not tell you, but we are vndone:

VVil. You must not tell me, but we are vndone,
Ile know the cause wherefore we are vndone.   *Exit vp.*

Rich Oh would the thing were but to doe againe,
The thought thereof doth rent my hart in twaine,

             Williams *to* Merry *aboue.*   *She goes vp.*

Wil. Oh maister, maister, what haue you done?

Mer. Why slaine a knaue that would haue murtherd
Better to kill, then to be kild my selfe.   (me.

Wil With what? wherewith? how haue you slaine the mã?

Mer. Why with this hammer I knockt out his braines.

VVil. Oh it was beastly so to butcher him,
If any quarrell were twixt him and you:
You should haue bad him meete you in the field,
Not like a coward vnder your owne roofe;
To knock him downe as he had bin an oxe,
Or silly sheepe prepard for slaughter house:
The Lord is iust, and will reuenge his blood,
On you and yours for this extremitie.
I will not stay an hower within your house,
It is the wickedst deed that ere was done.

Mer. Oh sir content your selfe, all shall be well,
Whats done already, cannot be vndone.

Rach. Oh would to God, the deéd were now to do,
And I were priuie to your ill intent,
You should not do it then for all the world.
But prethie *Harry* do not leaue the house,

                                        For

For then fuspition will arife thereof,
And if the thing be knowne we are vndone.

VVil. Forfake the houfe, I will not ftay all night,
Though you will giue the wealth of Chriftendome.

Mer. But yet conceale it, for the loue of God,
If otherwife, I know not what to do.

VVil. Here is my hand, ile neuer vtter it,
Affure your felfe of that, and fo farewell.

Mer. But fweare to me, as God fhall helpe thy foule,
Thou wilt not tell it vnto any one.

VVil. I will not fweare, but take my honeft worde,
And fo farewell, my foule affureth me,   *Exit Merry*
God will reuenge this damn'd iniquitie.   *and Rach.*
What fhall become of me vnhappie wretch?
I dare not lodge within my Maifters houfe,
For feare his murthrous hand fhould kill me too,
I will go walke and wander vp and downe,
And feeke fome reft, vntill the day appeare:
At the Three-Cranes, in fome Haye loft Ile lye,
And waile my Maifters comming miferie.   *Exit.*

Enter Fallerio *folus.*

Fal. I haue poffeffion of my brothers goods,
His tennants pay me rent, acknowledge me
To be their Landlord, they frequent my houfe,
With Turkeys, Capons, Pigeons, Pigges and Geefe,
And all to gaine my fauour and good will.
His plate, his Iewels, hangings, houfhould ftuffe,
May well befeeme to fit a demie King,
His ftately buildings, his delightfull walkes,
His fertile Meadowes, and rich ploughed lands,
His well growne woods and ftor'd Fifhing ponds,
Brings endleffe wealth, befides continuall helpe,
To keepe a good and hofpitable houfe:
And fhall I toy thefe pleafures but a time,
Nay brother, fifter, all fhall pardon me,
Before Ile fell my felfe to penurie.

C

The

The world doth know,thy brother but refign'd,
The lands and goods,vntill his fonne attain'de,
To riper yeares to weld and gouerne them,
Then openly thou canft not do him wrong,
He liuing : there's the burthen of the fong.
Call it a burthen,for it feemes fo great
And heauie burthen,that the boy fhould liue,
And thruft me from this height of happineffe:
That I will not indure fo heauie waight,
But fhake it off,and liue at libertie,
Free from the yoake of fuch fubiection,
The boy fhall dye,were he my fathers fonne,
Before Ile part with my poffeffion.
Ile call my fonne,and aske his good aduice,
How I may beft difpatch this ferious caufe:
Hoe fir *Allenfo* · *Alls*. Father. *Fall*. Hearken fonne,
I muft intreate your furtherance and aduife,
About a thing that doth concerne vs neere,
Firft tell me how thou dooft affect in heart,
Little *Pertillo*, thy dead Ynckles fonne.

   Allen. So well good father,that I cannot tell,
Whether I loue him dearer then my felfe :
And yet if that my heart were calde to count,
I thinke it would furrender me to death,
Ere young *Pertillo* fhould fuftaine a wrong.

   Fall. How got his fafetie fuch a deepe regarde
Within your heart,that you affect it fo?

   Allen. Nature gaue roote,loue,and the dying charge,
Of his dead father,giues fuch ftore of fap,
Vnto this tree of my affection,
That it will neuer wither till I dye.

   Fall. But nature,loue, and reafon,tels thee thus,
Thy felfe muft yet be neereft to thy felfe.

   Allen, His loue dooth not eftrange me from my felfe,
But doth confirme my ftrength with multitudes,
Of benefits,his loue will yeelde to me.

   Fall. Beware to fofter fuch pernicious fnakes,

                      With

Within thy bofome, which will poyfon thee.

Allyn He is a Doue, a childe, an innocent,
And cannot poyfon, father though he would.

Fall. I will be plainer, know *Pertillos* life,
Which thou dooft call, a Doue, an innocent:
A harmleffe childe, and, and I know not what,
Will harme thee more, then any Serpent can,
I, then the very fight of Bafiliskes.

Allen. Father, you tell me of a ftrange difcourfe,
How can his life produce fuch detriment,
As Bafiliskes, whofe onely fight is death?

Fall. Harken to me, and I will tell thee how:
Thou know ft his fathers goods, his houfes, lands,
Haue much aduaunc'd our reputation,
In hauing but their vfage for a time,
If the boy liue, then like to fenceleffe beafts,
Like longd eard Affes, and riche laden Mules,
We muft refigne thefe treafures to a boye,
And we like Affes feede on fimple Haye:
Make him away, they fhall continue ours,
By vertue of his fathers Teftament,
The Iewels, caftles, medowes, houfes, lands,
Which thy fmall cozen, fhould defeate thee of,
Be ftill thine owne, and thou aduance thy felfe,
Aboue the height of all thine Aunceftours.

Allen. But if I mount by murther and deceite,
Iuftice will thruft afpiring thoughts belowe,
And make me caper forto breake my neck:
After fome wofull lamentation,
Of my obedience to vnlawfulneffe:
I tell you plaine, I would not haue him dye,
Might I enioy the *Soldans* Emperie.

Fall. What wilt thou barre thy felfe of happineffe,
Stop the large ftreame of pleafures which would flowe,
And ftill attend on thee like Seruingmen:
Preferre the life of him that loues thee not,
Before thine owne, and my felicitie.

Allen.

Allen. Ide rather choose to feede on carefulnesse,
To ditche, to delue, and labour for my bread,
Nay rather choose to begge from doore to doore,
Then condiscend to offer violence,
To young *Pertillo* in his innocence,
I know you speake, to sound what mightie share,
Pertillo hath in my affection.

Fall. In faith I do not, therefore prethie say,
Wilt thou consent to haue him made away.

Allen. Why then in faith, I am ashamde to thinke,
I had my being from so foule a lumpe
Of adulation and vnthankfulnesse,
Ah, had their dying praiers no auaile
Within your hart? no, damnd extorcion,
Hath left no roome for grace to harbor in,
Audacious sinne, how canst thou make him say,
Consent to make my brothers sonne away.

Fall. Nay if you ginne to brawle, withdraw your selfe,
But vtter not the motion that I made,
As you loue me, or do regarde your life.

Allen. And as you loue my safetie, and your soule,
Let grace, and feare of God, such thoughts controule.

Fall. Still pratling, let your grace and feare alone,
And leaue me quickly to my priuate thoughts,
Or, with my sworde Ile open wide a gate,
For wrath and bloudie death to enter in.

Allen. Better you gaue me death and buriall,
Then such foule deeds should ouerthrow vs all.

Fall. Still are you wagging that rebellious tounge,
Ile dig it out for Crowes to feede vpon,
If thou continue longer in my sight.   *Exit Allenso.*
He loues him better then he loues his life,
Heres repetition of my brothers care,
Of sisters chardge, of grace, and feare of God,
Feare dastards, cowards, faint hart run-awayes,
Ile feare no coulours to obteine my will,
Though all the fiends in hell were opposite,

                                        Ide

Ide rather loofe mine eye, my hand, my foote,
Be blinde, wante fences, and be euer lame,
Then be tormented with fuch difcontent,
This refignation would afflict me with,
Be blithe my boy, thy life fhall fure be done,
Before the fetting of the morrowe funne.

Enter Auarice *and* Homicide *bloody.*

Hom: Make haft, runne headlong to deftruction,
I like thy temper, that canft change a heart,
From yeelding flefh, to Flinte and Adamant,
Thou hitft it home, where thou dooft faften holde,
Nothing can feperate the loue of golde.

Aua. Feare no relenting, I dare pawne my foule,
(And thats no gadge, it is the diuels due)
He fhall imbrew his greedie griping hands,
In the dead bofome of the bloodie boy,
And winde himfelfe, his fonne, and harmleffe wife,
In endleffe foldes of fure deftruction.
Now *Homicide,* thy lookes are like thy felfe,
For blood, and death, are thy companions,
Let my confounding plots but goe before,
And thou fhalt wade vp to the chin in gore.

Hom. I finde it true, for where thou art let in,
There is no fcrupule made of any finne,
The world may fee thou art the roote of ill,
For but for thee, poore *Beech* had liued ftill.   *Exeunt.*

Enter Rachel *and* Merry.

Rach. Oh my deare brother, what a heape of woe,
Your rafhneffe hath powrd downe vpon your head:
Where fhall we hide this trumpet of your fhame,
This timeleffe ougly map of crueltie?
Brother, if *VVilliams* do reueale the truth,
Then brother, then, begins our fceane of ruthe.

Mer. I feare not *VVilliams,* but I feare the boy,
Who knew I fetcht his maifter to my houfe.

Rach. What doth the boy know wherabouts you dwel?

Mer. I that tormentes me worſe then panges of hell,
He muſt be ſlaine to, elſe hele vtter all.

Rach. Harke brother, harke, me thinkes I here on call.

Mer. Go downe and ſee, pray God my man keep cloſe:
If he proue long-tongd then my daies are done,
The boy muſt die, there is no helpe at all:
For on his life, my verie life dependes,
Beſides I cannot compaſſe what I would,
Vnleſſe the boy be quicklie made away,
This that abridgde his hapleſſe maiſters daies,
Shall leaue ſuch ſound memorials one his head,
That he ſhall quite forget who did him harme,
Or train'd his maiſter to this bloodie feaſt:
Why how now *Rachell?* who did call below?

Enter Rachell.

Rach. A maide that came to haue a pennie loafe.

Mer. I would a pennie loafe coſt me a pound,
Prouided *Beeches* boy had eate his laſt.

Rach. Perchaunce the boy doth not remember you.

Mer. It maie be ſo, but ile remember him.   *to people.*
And ſend him quicklie with a bloodie ſcrowle,
To greete his maiſter in another world.

Rach. Ile goe to *Beeches* on a faind excuſe,
To ſee if he will aske me for his maiſter.

Mer. No, get you vp, you ſhall not ſtir abroade,
And when I call, come quicklie to the dore.

Rach. Brother, or that, or any thing beſide,
To pleaſe your minde, or eaſe your miſerie.   *Exit.*

Mer. I am knee deepe, ile wade vp to the waſt,
To end my hart of feare, and to attaine,
The hoped end of my intention?
But I maie ſee, if I haue eyes to ſee,
And if my vnderſtanding be not blind,
How manie dangers do alreadie waight,
Vpon my ſteppes of bold ſecuritie,
Williams is fled, perchaunce to vtter all,
Thats but perchance, naie rather flatlie no,

But

But should he tell, I can but die a death,
Should he conceale, the boy would vtter it,
The boy must die, there is no remedie.

The boy sitting at his maisters dore.

VVin. I wonder that my maister staies so long,
He had not wont to be abroade so late:
Yonder comes one, I thinke that same is he.

Mer. I see the boye sits at his maisters doore,
Or now, or neuer, *Merry* stir thy selfe,
And rid thy hart from feare and iealousie:
Thomas Winchester go quicklie to your shoppe,
What sit you still, your maister is at hand.

When the boy goeth into the shoppe Merrie *striketh
six blowes on his head & with the seauenth leaues
the hammer sticking in his head, the boy groaning
must be heard by a maide who must crye to her
maister.* Merrie *flieth.*

Mai. Oh God I thinke theres theeues in *Beeches* shop.

*Enter one in his shirt and a maide, and comming to
Beeches shop findes the boy murthered.*

Nei. What cruell hand hath done so foule a deede,
Thus to bemangle a distressed youth:
Without all pittie or a due remorse,
See how the hammer sticketh in his head,
Wherewith this honest youth is done to death,
Speake honest *Thomas*, if any speach remaine,
What cruell hand hath done this villanie:
He cannot speake, his sences are bereft,
Hoe neighbour *Loney*, pray come downe with speede,
Your tennant *Beeches* man is murthered.

Loney sleeping. What would you haue some Mustard?

Nei. Your tennant *Beeches* man, is murthered.

Lo. Whose smothered, I thinke you lack your wit, *Out*
What neighbor what make you here so late? *at a window*

Nei. I was affrighted by a sodaine crie,
And comming downe found maister *Beeches* man,
Thus with a hammer sticking in his head. *Comes downe.*

C 4   *Loney.*

Lowry. Ah wo is me for *Thomas Winchester,*
The truest soule that euer maister had,
Wheres maister *Beech? Neigh.* Nay, no body can tell:
Did you see any running from the dore,
When you lookt out and heard the youngman crie,

Maid. Yes I saw two trulie to my thinking, but they
Ranne away as fast as their hands could beare them:
By my troth twas so darke I could see no bodie, *To people.*
Pray God maister *Beech* hath not hurt his boy in his pati-
And if he haue he must be hangd in his choller. (ence

Lo. I dare be sworne he would not strike him thus,
Praie God his maister be not slaine himselfe.
The night growes late, and we will haue this course
Be watch'd all night, to morrow we shall see,
Whence sprang this strange vnciuill crueltie.

Nei. Neighbour good night. *Lon.* Neighbors all good
Mo. Praie God I neuer see so sad a sight. (night.

Exeunt omnes.

Enter Merry *knocking at the doore, and* Rachell
comes down:.

Mer. Oh sister, sister, now I am pursu'd,
The mightie clamour that the boy did make,
Hath raisde the neighbours round about the street:
So that I know not where to hide my selfe.

Ra. What brother, haue you kild *Beeches* boy?

Mer. No, no, not I, but yet another hath,
Come, come to bed, for feare we be discri'd:
The fearefullest night that euer *Merry* knew. *Exeunt.*

Enter Falleria *and two* Ruffaines.

Fall Seeme it not strange resolued gentleman,
That I thus p iuatelie haue seuered you, .
To open secret sorrowes of my hart:
Thinke not I do intend to vndermine,
Your passed liues, although you know I am,
A man to whom the true vnpartiall sworde,
Of equall iustice is deliuered,
Therefore sweare both, as you respect your soules,

A 3

At the laſt dreadfull ſeſſions held in heauen,
Firſt to conceale, and next to execute,
What I reueale, and ſhall enioyne you to.

   Both So you rewarde vs, whatſoeuer it be,
We vowe performance, and true ſecreſie.

   Fall. There go aſide, yee ſeeming ſemblances,
Of equall iuſtice, and true pietie,
And lay my hearts corrupted Cytadell,
Wide open to your thoughts to looke into.
Know I am nam'd *Fallerio*, to deceiue
The world with ſhew of truth and honeſtie,
But yet nor truth, nor honeſtie abides,
Within my thoughts, but falſhood, crueltie,
Blood ſucking *Auarice*, and all the ſinnes,
That hale men on to bloodie ſtratagems,
Like to your ſelues, which care not how you gaine,
By blood, extorcion, falſhood, periurie,
So you may haue a pleaſing recompence: *They ſtart.*
Start not aſide, depart not from your ſelues,
I know your compoſition is as mine,
Of bloud, extortion, falſhood, periurie,
True branded with the marke of wickedneſſe.

   1. Ruffin. Be not ſo bitter, we are they indeede,
That would depriue our fathers of their liues,
So we were ſure to haue a benefit :
I way no more the murthring of a child,
Drag'd from the ſucking boſome of his mother,
Then I reſpect to quaffe a boule of wine,
Vnto his health, that dearely loueth me.

   2 Ruff. Where golde rewardeth, were apparent death
Before mine eyes, bolde, hartie, viſible,
Ide wraſtle with him for a deadly fall,
Or I would looſe my guerdon promiſed :
Ide hang my brother for to weare his coate,
That all that ſawe me might haue cauſe to ſay,
There is a hart more firme then Adamant,
To practiſe execrable butcheries.

Fall. I know that well, for were I not assur'd,
Of your performance in this enterprice,
I would not ope the closet of my breft,
To let you know my close intention,
There is a little boy, an vrchin lad,
That ftands betweene me and the glorious rayes,
Of my foule-wiffing funne of happineffe:
There is a thicket ten miles from this place,
Whofe fecret ambuff, and vnvfed wayes,
Doth feeme to ioyne with our confpiracie,
There murther him, and when the deed is done,
Caft his dead body in fome durtie ditch,
And leaue him for the Fowles to feed vpon :
Do this, here is two hundreth markes in golde,
To harten on your refolution :
Two hundreth more, after the deed is done,
Ile pay you more for fatiffaction.

  1. Ruff. Swones her's rewards would make one kill him-
To leaue his progenie fo rich a prize,   (felfe,
Were twentie liues engadged for this coine,
Ide end them all, to haue the money mine.

  2. Ruff. Who would not hazard life, nay foule and all,
For fuch a franke and bounteous pay-maifter,
Sblood, what labour is't to kill a boy,
It is but thus, and then the taske is done,
It grieues me moft, that when this taske is paft,
I haue no more to occupie my felfe,
Two hundreth markes to giue a paltrie ftab,
I am impacient till I fee the brat.

  Fall. That muft be done with cunning fecrecie,
I haue deuifde to fend the boye abroade,
With this excufe, to haue him foftred,
In better manners then this place affoords,
My wife, though loath indeed to part with him,
Yet for his good, fhe will forgoe her ioy,
With hope in time to haue more firme delights,
Which fhe expects from young *Pertillos* life.

                                                      2. Ruff.

2. *Ruff.* Call you him *Perillo*, faith leaue out the *T*.

Fall. Why so?   *Ruff.* Becaufe *Perillo* will remaine,
For he fhall furely perifh if I liue :
What do you call the father of the child ?

Fall. Why man, he hath no father left aliue.

1. *Ruff.* Yes fuch a father, that doth fee and know,
How we do plot this little infants woe.   *To the people.*

2. *Ruff.* Why then his little fonne is much to blame,
That doth not keepe his father company.
When fhall we haue deliuerie of the boy ?

Fall. To morrow morning by the breake of day,
And you muft fweare youle fee him fafely brought,
Vnto the place that I do fend him to.

2 *Ruff.* That may we fafely, for you meane to fend
Him to the wood, and there his iourney ends:
Both foule and limbes fhall haue a place to reft,
In earth the laft, the firft in *Abrams* breft.

Fall. Come gentlemen, this night go reft with me,
To morrow end *Perillos* tragedie.   *Exeunt omnes.*

Enter Merry and Rachell.

Mer. Sifter, now all my golde expected hopes,
Of future good, is plainely vanifhed,
And in her ftead, grim vifadged difpaire,
Hath tane poffeffion of my guiltie heart,
Defire to gaine, began this defperate acte,
Now plaine apparance of deftruction,
Of foule and body, waights vpon my finne,
Although we hide our finnes from mortall men,
Whofe glaffe of knowledge is the face of man,
The eye of heauen beholdes our wickednesse,
And will no doubt reuenge the innocent.

Rach. Ah, do not fo difconfolate your felfe,
Nor adde new ftreames of forrow to your griefe,
Which like a fpring tide ouer-fwels the bankes,
Leaft you do make an inundation,
And fo be borne away with fwifteft tides,

D 2   Of

Of vgly feare, and ſtrong diſpairing thoughts,
I am your ſiſter, though a ſilly Maide,
Ile be your true and faithfull comforter.

Mer. Rachel, I ſee thy loue is infinite,
And ſorrow had ſo borne my thoughts away,
That I had almoſt quite forgot my ſelfe,
Helpe me deare ſiſter to conuey from hence,
The ſpectacle of inhumanitie.

Rach. Whether would you conuey this lumpe of duſt,
Vntimely murthred by your luckleſſe hand.

Mer. To the lowe roome, where we will couer it,
With Fagots, tell the euening doe approche:
In the meane time I will bethinke my ſelfe,
How I may beſt conuey it foorth of doores,
For if we keepe it longer in the houſe,
The ſauour will be felt throughout the ſtreete,
Which will betray vs to deſtruction.
Oh what a horror brings this beaſtlineſſe,
This chiefe of ſinnes, this ſelfe accuſing crime
Of murther: now I ſhame to know my ſelfe,
That am eſtrang'd ſo much from that I was,
True, harmleſſe, honeſt, full of curteſie,
Now falſe, deceitfull, full of iniurie:
Hould thou his heeles, ile beare his wounded head,
Would he did liue, ſo I my ſelfe were dead.

Bring downe the body, and couer it ouer with
Faggots, himſelfe.

Rach. Thoſe little ſtickes, do hide the murthred courſe,
But ſtickes, nor ought beſides, can hide the ſinne:
He ſits on high, whoſe quick all ſeeing eye,
Cannot be blinded by mans ſubtilties.

Mer. Looke euery where, can you diſcerne him now?
Rach. Not with mine eye, but with my heart I can.
Mer. That is becauſe thou knoweſt I laide him there,
To guiltineſſe each thought begetteth feare:
But go my true, though wofull comforter,
Wipe vp the blood in euery place aboue,

S⸱

So that no drop be found about the house,
I know all houses will be searcht anon :
Then burne the clothes, with which you wipe the ground
That no apparant signe of blood be found.

Rach. I will, I will, oh would to God I could
As cleerely wash your conscience from the deed,
As I can cleanse the house from least suspect,
Of murthrous deed, and beastly crueltie.

Mer. Cease to wish vainely, let vs seeke to saue,
Our names, our fames, our liues, and all we haue. *Exeunt.*

Enter three or foure neighbours together

1. *Neigh.* Neighbours, tis bruted all about the towne,
That *Robert Beech* a honest Chaundelor,
Had his man deadly wounded yester night,
At twelue a clock, when all men were a sleepe.

2. Where was his maister, when the deed was done.

3. No man can tell, for he is missing to,
Some men suspect that he hath done the fact,
And that for feare the man is fled away,
Others, that knew his honest harmlesse life,
Feare that himselfe is likewise made away.

4. Then let commaundement euery where be giuen,
That sinkes and gutters, priuies, creuises,
And euery place, where blood may be concea'ld,
Be throughly searcht, swept, washt, and neerely sought,
To see if we can finde the murther out :
And least that *Beech* be throwne into the *Thames,*
Let charge be giuen vnto the Watermen,
That if they see the body of a man,
Floting in any place about the *Thames,*
That straight they bring it vnto *Lambert hill,*
Where *Beech* did dwell when he did liue in health.

1. *Neigh.* Ile see this charge performd immediatly.

4. Now let vs go to Maister *Beeches* shop,   *Exit.*
To see if that the boy can giue vs light,
Of those suspitions which this cause doth yeeld.

2. This is the house call maister *Loney* forth,

3. Hoe maister *Loney*, doth the boy yet liue, *Ent. Loney*
Or can he vtter who hath done him wrong.

Lo. He is not dead but hath a dying life,
For neither speech, nor any sence at all,
Abideth in the poore vnhappie youth.

4. Here you of anie where his maister is.

Lo. No would we could, we all that knew his life,
Suspect him not for any such offence.

4. Bring forth the boy, that we may see his wounds.

> *Bringes him forth in a chaire, with a hammer
> sticking in his head.*

What say the Surgions to the yongmans woundes,

Lo. They giue him ouer, saying euerie wound
Of sixe, whereof ther's seauen in his head,
Are mortall woundes and all incurable.

> *They suruey his woundes.*

Enter Merrie, *and* Williams.

Mer. How now good *Harry*, hast thou hid my fault?
The boy that knew I train'd his maister forth:
Lies speechlesse, and euen at the point of death,
If you proue true, I hope to scape the brunt,

Will. Whie feare not me, I haue conceal'd it yet,
And will conceale it, haue no doubt of me.

Mer. Thankes gentle *Harry*, thou shalt neuer lacke,
But thou and I will liue as faithfull friendes,
And what I haue, shalbe thine owne to vse:
There is some monie for to spend to day,
I know you meane to goe and see the faire.

Wil. I faine would go, but that I want a cloake.

Mer. Thou shalt not want a cloake, or ought beside,
So thou wilt promise to be secret: *Giue him his cloake.*
Here take my cloake, ile weare my best my selfe,
But where did you lie this last night?

Wil. At the three Cranes, in a Carmans hay-loft,
But ile haue better lodging soone at night,

Mer.

Mer. Thou wilt be secret, I will go and see, *Exit Willi.*
What stir they keepe about *Beeches* shop,
Because I would auoyde suspition.   *Go to them.*
God saue you gentlemen, is this the boy
That is reported to be murthered?

    4. He is not dead outright, but pleas'd it God,
Twere better he had left this wicked world,
Then to liue thus in this extremitie.

    Mer. A cruell hand no doubt that did the deede,
Whie pull you not the hammer from his head.

    4. That must not be before the youth be dead,
Because the crowner and his quest may see,
The manner how he did receiue his death:
Beare hence the bodie, and endeuor all,
To finde them out that did the villanie.

             Exeunt omnes : manet Merrie.

    Mer. Do what you can, cast all your wits about,
Rake kennells, gutters, seeke in euerie place,
Yet I will ouergoe your cunning heads,
If *VVilliams* and my sister hold their tongues:
My neighbours holdes not me in least suspect,
Weighing of my former conuersation:
Were *Beeches* boy well conueid awaie,
Ide hope to ouerblow this stormie day.   *Exit.*

    Enter Falleria, Sostrata, Allenso, Pertillo : *and*
        two Murtherers booted.

    Fall. Now little cooze, you are content to goe
From me your vnckle and your louing Aunt,
Your faithfull cozen and your dearest friendes:
And all to come to be a skilfull man,
In learned artes and happie sciences.

    Per. I am content, because it pleaseth you,
My father bid I should obey your will,
And yeelde my selfe to your discretion;
Besides my cozen gaue me yesternight,
A prettie Nag to ride to *Padua,*

        D 4 .   Of

Of all my friends *Alleaso* loues me best.

 Full. I thinke thou art infpir'd with prophefie, *To the*
He loues thee better then I would he did: *people.*
Why wherefore thinke you fo my pretie Nephew?

 Per Becaufe he taught me how to fay my prayers,
To ride a horfe, to ftart the fearefull Hare,
He gaue this dagger to me yefter night,
This little Ring, and many pretie things:
For which, kinde cooze, I reft your true debtor,
And one day I will make you recompence.

 Fall. I, with thy lands and goods thou leau'ft behinde.

 Alen. Pray father let me go along with him:
Now by the fauiour of my finfull foule,   *To the people.*
I do not like thofe fellowes countenance.

 Fill. Sonne be content, weele go a feauenight hence,
And fee him in his vniuerfitie weedes :
Thefe will conduct him fafely to the place,
Be well affured they'l haue a care of him,
That you fhall neuer fee *Pertillo* more.   *To the people.*

 Allen. Father, I pray you to withdraw your felfe,
Ide haue a word or two in fecrefie. *They fpeake together.*

 Soft. Come liuing image of thy dead mother,
And take my louing farewell, ere we part,
I loue thee dearly for thy fathers fake,
But for thy mothers, doate with iealoufie,
Oh I do feare, before I fee thy face,
Or thou, or I, fhall tafte of bitterneffe :
Kiffe me fweete boy, and kiffing folde thine Aunte,
Within the circle of thy little armes,
I neede not feare, death cannot offer wrong,
The maieftie of thy prefaging face,
Would vanquifh him though nere fo terrible,
The angrie Lioneffe that is bereau'd,
Of her imperious crew of forreft kings,
Would leaue her furie and defend thee fafe,
From Wolues, from Panthers, Leopards, and fhee Beares,
That liue by rapine, ftealth, and crueltie,

           There-

Therefore to God I do commend thy ſtate,
Who will be ſure to guarde thee tenderly.
And now to you,that carry hence this wealth,
This precious iewell,this vnprized good,
Haue a regarde to vſe him carefully,
When he is parted from that ſerious care,
Which was imployde for his ſecuritie:
I vrge it not,that I miſdoubt your truth,
I hope his Vnckle doth perſwade himſelfe,
You will be courteous,kinde and affable,
Ther's ſome rewarde for hoped carefulneſſe.

 Allen. Now by my ſoule I do ſuſpect the men,
Eſpecially the lower of the two :
See what a hollow diſcontented looke,
He caſts,which brings apparant cauſe of feare,
The other,though he ſeeme more courteous,
Yet dooth his lookes preſadge this thought in me,
As if he ſcorn'd to thinke on courteſie.

 Fall. Vpon my life,my ſonne you are to blame,
The gentlemen are honeſt,vertuous,
And will protect *Pertillo* happily :
Theſe thoughts proceed out of aboundant loue,
Becauſe you grieue to leaue his company:
If ought betide him otherwiſe then well,
Let God require due vengaunce on my head,
And cut my hopes from all proſperitie.

 Allen. A heauie ſentence,full of wondrous feare,
I cannot chooſe but credit ſuch a vowe,
Come hether then,my ioy,my chiefeſt hopes.
My ſecond ſelfe,my earthly happineſſe,
Lend me thy little prety cherry lip,
To kiſſe me cozen,lay thy little hand
Vpon my cheeke,and hug me tenderly,
Would the cleere rayes of thy two glorious ſunnes,
Could penetrate the corners of my heart,
That thou might ſee,how much I tender thee.
My friends beholde within this little bulke,

E

Two

Two perfect bodyes are incorporate,
His life holdes mine, his heart conteines my hart,
His euery lim, containes my euery part:
Without his being, I can neuer be,
He being dead, prepare to burie me.
Oh thou immortall mouer of the spheares,
Within their circled reuolusions,
Whose glorious image this small orphant beares,
Wrought by thy all sufficient Maiestie,
Oh neuer suffer any wicked hand,
To harme this heauenly workmanship of thine,
But let him liue, great God to honour thee,
With vertuous life, and spotlesse pietie.

Per. Cease my kinde cooze, I cannot choose but weepe,
To see your care of my securitie.

Allen. Knewst thou my reason, that perswades my hart,
Thou wouldst not wonder, why I grieue to part:
But yet I would suspect my fathers vowe,
Did any other make it by your leaue.

Fall. What haue you done, this lothnesse to depart,
Seemes you were trained vp in rediousnesse,
That know not when and where to make an end:
Take him my friends, I know you will discharge,
The hope and trust that I repose in you.

Both. Assure your selfe, in euery circumstance.

Fall. Then to your horses, quicklie, speedily,
Else we shall put our fingers in the eye,
And weepe for kindnesse till to morrow morne.

Per, Farewell good Vnckle, Aunt and louing cooze.

Softratus kisseth the boy weeping.

Allen. Farewell, I feare me euerlastinglie.

Exeunt Softratus *and* Allenso.

One of the murtherers takes Falleria *by the*
sleeue.

1. mu. You meane not now to haue him murthered?

Fall. Not murthered, what else? kill him I say,
But wherefore makest thou question of my will?

Mur.

Mur. Becaufe you wifht that God fhould be reueng'd
If any ill betide the innocent.

Fall. Oh that was nothing but to blind the eyes,
Of my fond fonne, which loues him too too well.

Mur, It is enough, it fhall be furely done. *Exeunt omi,*

  Enter Merry *and* Rachel *with a bag.*

Mer. What haft thou fped ? haue you bought the bag ?
Rach. I brother, here it is, what is't to do ?
Mer. To beare hence *Beeches* body in the night.
Rach. You cannot beare fo great a wayght your felfe,
And 'tis no trufting of another man.
Mer. Yes well enough, as I will order it,
Ile cut him peece-meale, firft his head and legs
Will be one burthen, then the mangled reft,
Will be another, which I will tranfport,
Beyond the water in a Ferry boate,
And throw it into *Paris-garden* ditch.
Fetch me the chopping-knife, and in the meane
Ile moue the Fagots that do couer him.
    Remooue the Fagots.
 Rach. Oh can you finde in hart to cut and carue,
His ftone colde flefh, and rob the greedy graue,
Of his diffeuered blood befprinckled lims ?
 Mer. I mary can I fetch the chopping knife.
 Rach This deed is worfe, thē whē you tooke his life. *Exit*
 Mer. But worfe, or better, now it muft be fo,
Better do thus, then feele a greater woe.
 Ent. Rach. Here is the knife, I cannot ftay to fee,
This barbarous deed of inhumanitie.   *Exit Rachel.*

   Merry *begins to cut the body, and bindes the armes*
    behinde his backe with Beeches *garters, leaues*
    out the body, couers the head and legs againe.

   Enter Truth.

Yee glorious beames of that bright-fhining lampe,
That lights the ftarre befpangled firmament,
     E 2   **And**

And dimnes the glimmering shadowes of the night,
Why doost thou lend assistance to this wretch,
To shamble forth with bolde audacitie,
His lims, that beares thy makers semblance.
All you the sad spectators of this Acte,
Whose harts do taste a feeling pensiuenesse,
Of this vnheard of sauadge Massacre :
Oh be farre of, to harbour such a thought,
As this audacious murtherer put in vre,
I see your sorrowes flowe vp to the brim,
And ouerflowe your cheekes with brinish teares,
But though this sight bring surfet to the eye,
Delight your eares with pleasing harmonie,
That eares may countercheche your eyes, and say,
Why shed you teares, this deede is but a playe:
His worke is done, he seekes to hide his sinne,
Ile waile his woe, before his woe begin. *Exit* Trueth.

   Mer. Now will I high me to the water side,
And fling this heauie burthen in a ditche,
Whereof my soule doth feele so great a waight,
That it doth almost presse me downe with feare,
                Enter Rachell.
Harke *Rachel* : I will crosse the water straight,
And fling this middle mention of a man,
Into some ditch, then high me home againe,
To rid my house of that is left behinde.
   Rach. Where haue you laide the legs & battered head?
   Mer. Vnder the fagots, where it lay before,
Helpe me to put this trunke into the bag.
   Rach. My heart will not endure to handle it,
The sight hereof doth make me quake for feare.
   Mer. Ile do't my selfe, onely drie vp the blood,
And burne the clothes as you haue done before. *Exit.*
   Rach. I feare thy soule will burne in flames of hell,
Vnlesse repentance wash away thy sinne,
With clensing teares of true contrition :
Ah did not nature ouersway my will,

                    The

The world should know this plot of damned ill.　*Exit*

Enter two Murtherers with Pertillo.

Per. I am so wearie in this combrous wood,
That I must needes go sit me downe and rest.

1. Mur. What were we best to kill him vnawares,
Or giue him notice what we doe intend?

2. Mur. Whie then belike you meane to do your charge
And feele no tast of pittie in your hart.

1. Mur Of pittie man, that neuer enters heere,
And if it should, Ide threat my crauen hart,
To stab it home, for harbouring such a thought,
I see no reason whie I should relent:
It is a charitable vertuous deede,
To end this princkocke from this sinfull world.

2. Mur. Such charitie will neuer haue reward,
Vnlesse it be with sting of conscience:
And that's a torment worse then *Sisipus*,
That rowles a restlesse stone against the hill.

1. Mur. My conscience is not prickt with such conceit.

2. Mur. That shews thee further off from hoped grace.

1. Mur. Grace me no graces, I respect no grace,
But with a grace, to giue a gracelesse stab,
To chop folkes legges and armes off by the stumpes,
To see what shift theile make to scramble home:
Pick out mens eyes, and tell them thats the sport,
Of hood-man-blinde, without all sportiuenesse,
If with a grace I can performe such pranckes,
My hart will giue mine agents many thankes.

2. Mur. Then God forbid I should consort my selfe,
With one so far from grace and pietie:
Least being found within thy companie,
I should be partner of thy punishment.

1. Mur. When wee haue done what we haue vow'd to
My hart desires to haue no fellowship,　(do,
With those that talke of grace or godlinesse:
I nam'd not God vnleast twere with an othe,
Sence the first houre that I could walke alone,

　(And

(And you that make so much of conscience,
By heauen thou art a damned hipocrite:
For thou hast vow'd to kill that sleeping boy,
And all to gaine two hundreth markes in gold,
I know this purenesse comes of pure deceit,
To draw me from the murthering of the child,
That you alone might haue the benefit,
You are too shallow, if you gull me so,
Chop of my head to make a Sowsing-tub,
And fill it full of tripes and chitterlinges.

   2. Mur. That thou shalt see my hart is far from fraud,
Or vaine illusion in this enterprize,
Which doth import the safetie of our soules,
There take my earnest of impietie.   *Giue him his mony.*
Onely forbeare to lay thy ruder handes,
Vpon the poore mistrustlesse tender child,
As for our vowes, feare not their violence,
God will forgiue on hartie penitence.

   1. Mur. Thou Eunuch, Capon, dastard, fast and loose,
Thou weathercocke of mutabilitie,
White luered Paisant, wilt thou vowe and sweare,
Face and make semblance with thy bagpipe othes,
Of that thou neuer meanst to execute?
Pure cowardice for feare to crack thy necke,
With the huge *Caos* of thy bodies waight,
Hath sure begot this true contrition,
Then fast and pray, and see if thou canst winne,
A goodlie pardon for thy hainous sinne,
As for the boy, this fatall instrument,
Was mark'd by heauen to cut his line of life,
And must supplie the knife of *Atropos*,
And if it doe not, let this maister peece,
(Which nature lent the world to wonder at)
Be slit in *Carbonadoes* for the iawes,
Of some men-eating hungrie *Canniball*:
By heauen ile kill him onely for this cause,
For that he came of vertuous Aunceltors,

                                   2. m. But

2 m. But by that God, which made that wondrous globe,
Wherein is seene his power full dietie,
Thou shalt not kill him mangre all thy spight.
Sweare, and forsweare thy selfe ten thousand times,
Awake *Pertulo*, for thou art betrai'd,
This bloody slaue intends to murther thee.   *Draw both.*
  1 mur. Both him, and all, that dare to rescue him.
      Per. Wherefore? because I slept without your leaue?
Forgiue my fault, Ile neuer sleepe againe.
      2 mur. No child, thy wicked Vnckle hath suborn'd,
Both him and me to take thy life away :
Which I would saue, but that this hellish impe,
Will not consent to spare thy guiltlesse blood.
      Per. Why should *Falleria* seeke to haue my life.
      2.mur. The lands and goods, thy father left his sonne,
Do hale thee on to thy destruction.
      Per. Oh needy treasure, harme begetting good,
That safely should procure the losse of blood.
      2.mu. Those lands and goods, thy father got with paine,
Are swords wherewith his little sonne is slaine.
      1.mu. Then let our swords let out his guiltlesse life.
      Per. Sweete, sowre, kinde, cruell, holde thy murthering
And here me speake, before you murther me.   (knife,
      2.mu. Feare not sweet child, he shall not murther thee.
      1.mu. No, but my sword shall let his puddings foorth.
      Per. First here me speake, thou map of Butcherie,
Tis but my goods and lands my Vnckle seekes,
Hauing that safely, he desires no more,
I do protest by my dead parents soules,
By the deare loue of false *Fallerios* sonne,
Whose heart, my heart assures me, will be grieu'd,
To heare his fathers inhumanitie :
I will forsake my countrie, goods, and lands,
I and my selfe, will euen change my selfe,
In name, in life, in habit, and in all,
And liue in some farre moued continent,
So you will spare my weake and tender youth,

                                        Which

Which cannot entertaine the ſtroake of death,
In budding yeares, and verie ſpring of life.

  1.Mur. Leaue of theſe bootleſſe proteſtations,
And vſe no ruth entiſing argumentes,
For if you doe, ile lop you lim by lim,
And torture you for childiſh eloquence.

  2.Mur. Thou ſhalt not make his little finger ake.

  1.Mur. Yes euery part,and this ſhall ptooue it true.

         Runnes Pertillo *in with his ſworde.*

  Per. Oh I am ſlaine,the Lord forgiue thy fact,
And giue thee grace to dye with penitence.   *Dyeth.*

  2.Mur. A treacherous villaine,full of cowardiſe,
Ile make thee know that thou haſt done amiſſe.

  1.m. Teach me that knowledge when you will or dare.

      *They fight and kill one another, the relenter hauing
      ſome more life,and the other dyeth.*

  1. mur. Swoones I am peppered,I had need haue ſalt,
Or elſe to morrow I ſhall yeeld a ſtincke,
Worſe then a heape of durty excrements :
Now by this Hilt,this golde was eam'd too deare :
Ah,how now death,wilt thou be conquerour ?
Then vengeance light on them that made me ſo,
And ther's another farewell ere I goe.

      Stab the other murtherer againe.

  2.mur. Enough,enough, I had my death before.

      A hunt within.

     Enter the Duke of Padua, Turqualo,Veſuvio,
         Alberto, *&c.*

  Duke. How now my Lords, was't not a gallant courſe.
Beleeue me ſirs, I neuer ſaw a wretch,
Make better ſhift to ſaue her little life ·
The thickets full of buskes and ſcratching bryers,
A mightie dewe,a many deepe mouth'd hounds,
Let looſe in euery place to croſſe their courſe,
And yet the Hare got cleanly from them all:
I would not for a hundred pound in faith,

                           But

But that she had escaped with her life,
For we will winde a merry hunters horne,
And start her once againe to morrow morne.

Tarq. In troth my Lord, the little flocked hound,
That had but three good legs to further him,
Twas formost still, and surer of his sent,
Then any one in all the crie besides.

Vesu. But yet *Pendragon* gaue the Hare more turnes.

Alber. That was because he was more pollitieke,
And eyed her closely in her couerts still:
They all did well, and once more we will trie,
The subtile creature with a greater crie.

Enter Allenso *booted.*

Duke. But say, what well accomplishd Gentleman,
Is this that comes into our company?

Vesu. I know him well, it is *Falerios* sonne,
Pandynos brother (a kinde Gentleman)
That dyed, and left his little pretty sonne,
Vnto his fathers good direction.

Duke. Stand close awhile, and ouer heare his wordes,
He seemes much ouer-gone with passion.

Alen. Yee timorous thoughts that guide my giddy steps,
In vnknowne pathes of dreadfull wildernesse,
Why traitor-like do you conspire to holde,
My pained heart, twixt feare and iealousie,
My too much care hath brought me carelesly,
Into this woody sauadge labyrinth,
And I can finde no waye to issue out,
Feare hath so dazeled all my better part,
That reason hath forgot discreations art:
But in good time, see where is company.
Kinde Gentlemen, if you vnlike my selfe,
Are not incumbred with the circling wayes,
Of this erronious winding wildernesse,
I pray you to direct me foorth this wood,
And shew the pathe that leades to *Padua.*

Duke. We all are *Paduans*, and we all intend,

.F

To passe forthwith, with speed to *Padua*.)

Allen. I will attend vpon you presently.   *See the bodyes.*

Duke. Come then away, but gentlemen beholde,
A bloody sight, and murtherous spectacle.

2. *Mur.* Oh God forgiue me all my wickednesse,
And take me to eternall happinesse.

Duke. Harke one of them hath some small sparke of life,
To kindle knowledge of their sad mishaps.

Alen. Ah gracious Lord, I know this wretched child,
And these two men that here lye murthered.

Vesu. Do you *Alenso* ?   *Allen.* I my gracious Lord:
It was *Pertillo* my dead Vnckles sonne :
Now haue my feares brought forth this fearefull childe,
Of endlesse care, and euerlasting griefe.

Duke. Lay hands vpon *Alenso* Gentlemen,
Your presence doth confirme you had a share,
In the performance of this crueltie.

Alen. I do confesse I haue so great a share,
In this mishap, that I will giue him thankes,
That will let foorth my sorrow wounded soule,
From out this goale of lamentation.

Duke. Tis now too late to wish for hadiwist,
Had you withheld your hand from this attempt,
Sorrow had neuer so imprisoned you.

Allen. Oh my good Lord, you do mistake my case,
And yet my griefe is sure infallible,
The Lord of heauen can witnesse with my soule,
That I am guildesse of your wrong suspect,
But yet not griefelesse that the deed is done.

Duke. Nay if you stand to iustifie your selfe,
This Gentleman whose life dooth seeme to stay,
Within his body tell he tell your shame,
Shall testifie of your integritie :
Speake then thou sad Anatomy of death,
Who were the agents of your wofulnesse.

2. *Mur.* O be not blinded with a false surmise,
For least my tongue should faile to end the tale.

Of our vntimely fate appointed death :
Know young *Allenso* is as innocent,
As is *Fallerio* guiltie of the crime.
He, he it was, that with foure hundreth markes,
Whereof two hundred he paide presently,
Did hire this damn'd villaine and my selfe,
To massacre this harmelesse innocent:
But yet my conscience toucht with some remorse,
Would faine haue sau'd the young *Pertilos* life,
But he remorselesse would not let him liue,
But vnawares thrust in his harmlesse brest,
That life bereauing fatall instrument:
Which cruell deede I seeking to reuenge,
Haue lost my life, and paid the slaue his due
Rewarde, for spilling blood of Innocents :
Surprise *Fallerio* author of this ill,
Saue young *Allenso*, he is guiltlesse still.   *Dyeth.*

Ailen. Oh sweetest honie mixt with bitter gall,
Oh Nightingale combinde with Rauens notes,
Thy speech is like a woodward that should say,
Let the tree liue, but take the roote away.
As though my life were ought but miserie,
Hauing my father slaine for infamie.

Duke. What should incite *Fallerio* to deuise,
The ouerthrowe of this vnhappie boy,.

Vesu. That may be easily guest my gracious Lord,
To be the lands *Pandino* left his sonne,
Which after that the boy were murthered,
Discend to him by due inheritance.

Duke. You deeme aright, see gentlemen the fruites,
Of coueting to haue anothers right,
Oh wicked thought of greedie couetice,
Could neither nature, feare of punishment,
Scandall to wife and children, nor the feare,
Of Gods confounding strict seueritie,
Allay the head-strong furie of thy will,
Beware my friends to wish vnlawfull gaine,

It

It will beget ftrange actions full of feare,
And ouerthrowe the actor vnawares,
For firft *Fallerios* life muft fatiffie,
The large effufion of their guiltleffe bloods,
Traind on by him to thefe ex-remities,
Next, wife and children muft be difpofeft,
Of lands and goods, and turnde to beggerie,
But moft of all, his great and hainous finne,
Will be an eye fore to his guiltleffe kinne.
Beare hence away thefe models of his fhame,
And let vs profecute the murtherer,
With all the care and dilligence we can.

      Two muft be carrying away Pertillo.

  Allen Forbeare a while, to beare away my ioy,
Whtch now is vanifht, fince his life is fled,
And giue me leaue to wafh his deadly wound,
With hartie teares, out-flowing from thofe eyes,
Which lou'd his fight, more then the fight of heauen:
Forgiue me God for this idolatrie.
Thou vgly monfter, grim imperious death,
Thou raw-bonde lumpe of foule deformitie.
Reguardleffe inftrument of cruell fate,
Vnparciall Sergeant, full of treacherie,
Why didft thou flatter my ill boding thoughts,
And flefh my hopes with vaine illufions:
Why didft thou fay, *Pertillo* fhould not dye,
And yet, oh yet, haft done it cruelly :
Oh but beholde, with what a fmiling cheere,
He intertain'd thy bloody harbinger:
See thou tranfformer of a heauenly face,
To Afhie paleneffe and vnpleafing lookes,
That his faire countenance ftill reteineth grace,
Of perfect beauty in the very graue,
The world would fay fuch beauty fhould not dye,
Yet like a theefe thou didft it cruelly :
Ah, had thy eyes deepe funke into thy head,
Beene able to perceiue his vertuous minde,

                      Where

Where vertue fate inthroned in a chaire,
With awfull grace, and pleafing maieftie:
Thou wouldeft not then haue let *Pertillo* die,
Nor like a theefe haue flaine, him cruellie.
Ineuitable fates, could you deuife,
No meanes to bring me to this pilgrimage,
Full of great woes and fad calamities,
But that the father fhould be principall,
To plot the prefent downfall of the fonne:
Come then kinde death and giue me leaue to die,
Since thou haft flaine *Pertillo* cruellie.

   Du. Forbeare *Allenfo* harken to my doome,
Which doth concerne thy fathers apprehenfion,
Firft we enioyne thee vpon paine of death,
To giue no fuccour to thy wicked fire,
But let him perrifh in his damned finne,
And pay the price of fuch a trecherie:
See that with fpeede the monfter be attach'd,
And bring him fafe to fuffer punifhment,
Preuent it not, nor feeke not to delude,
The officers to whom this charge is giuen,
For if thou doe, as fure as God doth liue :
Thy felfe fhall fatiffie the lawes contempt,
Therefore forward about this punifhment.

Exeunt omnes manet Allenfo.

   Al. Thankes gratious God that thou haft left the meanes
To end my foule from this perplexitie,
Not fuccour him on paine of prefent death:
That is no paine, death is a welcome gueft,
To thofe whofe harts are ouerwhelm'd with griefe,
My woes are done, I hauing leaue to die,
And after death liue euer ioyfullie. *Exit.*

Enter Murther and Couetoufneffe.

   Mur. Now *Auarice* I haue well fatiffied,
My hungry thoughtes with blood and crueltie:
Now all my melanchollie difcontent,

F 3 Is

Is shaken of, and I am throughlie pleaf'd,
With what thy pollicie hath brought to paffe,
Yet am I not fo throughlie fatiffied:
Vntill I bring the purple actors forth,
And caufe them quaffe a bowle of bitterneffe,
That father, fonne, and fifter brother may,
Bring to their deathes with moft affur'd decay.

   Ana. That wilbe done without all queftion,
For thou haft flaine *Allenfo* with the boy:
And *Rachell* doth not wifh tooouerliue,
The fad remembrance of her brothers finne,
Leaue faithfull loue, to teach them how to dye,
That they may fhare their kinffolkes miferie.   *Exeunt.*

   Enter Merrie *and* Rachell *vncouering the*
     head and legges.

   Mer. I haue beftow'd a watrie funerall,
On the halfe bodie of my butchered friend,
The head and legges Ile leaue in fome darke place,
I care not if they finde them yea or no.

   Ra. Where do you meane to leaue the head and legs,

   Mer. In fome darke place nere to Bainardes caftle,

   Ra. But doe it clofelie that you be not feene,
For all this while you are without fufpect.

   Mer. Take you no thought, ile haue a care of that,
Onelie take heede you haue a fpeciall care,
To make no fhew of any difcontent,
Nor vfe too many words to any one.
          Puts on his cloake taketh vp the bag.
I will returne when I haue left my loade,
Be merrie *Rachell* halfe the feare is paft.

   Ra. But I fhall neuer thinke my felfe fecure,   *Exit.*
This deede would trouble any quiet foule,
To thinke thereof, much more to fee it done,
Such cruell deedes can neuer long be hid,
Although we practice nere fo cunningly.
                           Let

Two Tragedies in one.

Let others open what I doe conceale,
Lo he is my brother, I will couer it,
And rather dye then haue it spoken rife,
Lo where fhe goes,betrai'd her brothers life.   *Exit.*

Enter Williams *and* Cowley.

Co. Why how now *Harry* what fhould be the caufe,
That you are growne fo difcontent of late :
Your fighes do fhew fome inward heauineffe,
Your heauy lookes, your eyes brimfull of teares,
Beares teftimonie of fome fecret griefe,
Reueale it *Harry*,I will be thy friend,
And helpe thee to my poore habillity.

Wil. If I am heauie,if I often figh,
And if my eyes beare recordes of my woe,
Condemne me not,for I haue mightie caufe,
More then I will impart to any one.

Co. Do you mifdoubt me, that you dare not tell
That woe to me, that moues your difcontent.

Wil. Good maifter *Cowley* you were euer kinde,
But pardon me, I will not vtter it,
To any one,for I haue paft my worde,
And therefore vrge me not to tell my griefe.

Cow. But thofe that fmother griefe too fecretly,
May waft themfelues in filent anguifhment,
And bring their bodies to fo low an ebbe,
That all the world can neuer make is flowe,
Vnto the happy highth of formei health:
Then be not iniurious to thy felfe,
To waft thy ftrength in lamentation,
But tell thy cafe,wele feeke fome remedie.

Wil. My caufe of griefe is now remedileffe,
And all the world can neuer leffen it,
Then fince no meanes can make my forrowes leffe,
Suffer me waile a woe which wants redreffe.

Cow. Yet let me beare a part in thy lamentes,
I loue thee not fo ill,but I will mone,

              F 4   Thy

Thy heauie haps, thou shalt not sigh alone.

Wil Nay, if you are so curious to intrude,
Your selfe to sorrow, where you haue no share,
I will frequent some vnfrequented place,
Where none shall here nor see my lamentations.

Cow. And I will follow where soeuer thou goe,   *Exit.*
I will be partner of thy helplesse woe.   *Exit.*

Enter two Watermen.

1. Wil ist not time we should go to our boates,
And giue attendance for this Bartlemew tide:
Folkes will be stirring early in the morning.

2. By my troth I am indifferent whether I go or no.
If a fare come why so, if not, why so, if I haue not their
money, they shall haue none of my labour.

1. But we that liue by our labours, must giue attendance,
But where lyes thy Boate?

2. At Baynards castle staires.

1. So do's mine, then lets go together.

2. Come, I am indifferent, I care not so much for going,
But if I go with you, why so: if not, why so.
        He falles ouer the bag.
Sblood what rascall hath laide this in my way?

1. A was not very indifferent that did so, but you are so
permentorie, to say, why so, and why so, that euery one is
glad to do you iniurie, but lets see, what is it?
        Taking the Sack by the end, one of the
        legs and head drops out.
Good Lord deliuer vs, a mans legges, and a head with manie wounds.

2. Whats that so much, I am indifferent, yet for mine
owne part, I vnderstand the miserie of it, if you doe, why
so, if not, why so.

1. By my troth I vnderstand no other mistery but this,
It is a strange and very rufull sight,
But prethee what doost thou conceit of it.

2 In troth I am indifferent, for if I tell you, why so, if not
        why

why so.

1. If thou tell me, Ile thanke thee, therefore I prithee
tell me.

2. I tell you I am indifferent, but to be plaine with you,
I am greeued to stumble at the hangmans budget.

1. At the hangmans budget, why this is a sack.

2. And to speake indifferently, it is the hang-mans
Budget, and because he thought too much of his labour to
set this head vpon the bridge, and the legs vpon the gates,
he flings them in the streete for men to stumble at, but if I
get him in my boate, Ile so belabour him in a stretcher,
that he had better be stretcht in one of his owne halfepeny
halters: if this be a good conceit, why so, if not, why so.

1. Thou art dec̄eiu'd, this head hath many wounds,
And hoase and shooes remaining on the legs,
Bull alwayes strips all quartered traitors quite.

2. I am indifferent whether you beleeue me or no,
these were not worth taking off, and therfore he left them
on, if this be likely why so, if not, why so.

1. Nay then I see you growe from worse to worse,
I heard last night, that one neere Lambert hill
Was missing, and his boye was murthered,
It may be this is a part of that same man:
What ere it be, Ile beare it to that place.

2. Masse I am indifferent, Ile go along with you,
If it be so, why so, if not why so. *Exeunt.*

Enter three neighbors knocking at Loneys
doore: Loney *comes.*

1. Hoe maister *Loney*, here you any newes,
What is become of your Tennant *Beech?*

Lon. No truely sir, not any newes at all.

2. What hath the boy recouered any speach,
To giue vs light of these suggestions,
That do arise vpon this accident.

Lon. There is no hope he should recouer speech,
The wiues do say, he's ready now to leaue

G   This

This greeuous world full fraught with treacherie,

3. Me thinkes if *Beech* himselfe be innocent,
That then the murtherer should not dwell farre off,
The hammer that is sticking in his head,
Was borrowed of a Cutler dwelling by,
But he remembers not, who borrowed it:
He is committed that did owe the hammer,
But yet he standes vppon his innocence,
And *Beeches* absence causeth great suspition.

Lo. If *Beech* be faulty, as I do not thinke,
I neuer was so much deceiu'd before,
Oh had you knowne his conuersation,
You would not haue him in suspition.

3. Diuels seeme Saints, and in this hatefull times,
Deceite can beate apparraunt signes of trueth,
And vice beare shew of vertues excellence.

Enter the two VVatermen.

1. I pray is this maister *Beeches* house?

Lo. My friend this same was maister *Beeches* shop,
We cannot tell whether he liue or no, I neth

1. Know you his head and if I shew it you,
Or can you tell what hose or shooes he ware,
At that same time when he forsooke the shoppe.

3. What haue you head, and hose, and shooes to show,
And want the body that should vse the same.

1. Behold this head, these legges, these hose and shooes,
And see if they were *Beeches* yea or no.

Lo. They are the same, alas what is become,
Of the remainder of this wretched man.

1. VVat. Nay that I know not, onelie these we found,
As we were comming vp a narrow lane,
Neere Baynardes Castle, where we two did dwell,
And heering that a man was missing hence,
We thought it good to bring these to this place, (paines,

3. Thankes my good friendes, ther's some thing for your

2. Wat. We are indifferet, whether you giue vs any thing
or nothing, and if you had not, why so, but since you haue,
why so.   1. Wat.

1.Wat. Leaue your repining sir we thanke you hartely.
3. Farewell good fellowes, neighbour now be bold,

Exeunt Watermen.

They dwell not farre that did this bloodie deed,
As God no doubt will at the last reueale:
Though they conceale it nere so cunninglie,
All houses, gutters, sincks and creuices,
Haue carefullie beene sought for, for the blood,
Yet theres no instaunce found in any place.

Enter a Porter and a gentleman.

But who is that, that brings a heauy loade,
Behinde him on a painefull porters backe.

Gen. Praie gentlemen which call you *Beeckes* shoppe?
3.Nei. This is the place, what weld you with the man?
Gen. Nothing with him, I heare the man is dead,
And if he be not, I haue lost my paines.
Lo. Hees dead indeede, but yet we cannot finde,
What is become of halfe his hopelesse bodie,
His head and legges are found but for the rest,
No man can tell what is become of it.
Gen. Then I doe thinke I can resolue your doubt,
And bring you certaine tydings of the rest,
And if you know his doublet and his shirt:
As for the bodie it is so abus'd,
That no man can take notice whoes it was,
Set downe this burthen of anothers shame,
What do you know the doublet and the shirt. *Ex. Porter.*
Lo. This is the doublet, these the seuered limmes,
Which late were ioyned to that mangled trunke:
Lay them together see if they can make,
Among them all a sound and solid matter.
3.neigh. They all agree, but yet they cannot make,
That sound and whole, which a remorsles hand
Hath seuered with a knife of crueltie:
But say good sir, where did you finde this out?
Gent Walking betime by Paris-garden ditch,
Hauing my Water Spaniell by my side,

G 2

When

When we approach'd vnto that haplesse place,
Where this same trunke lay drowned in a ditch,
My Spaniell gan to sent, to barke, to plunge,
Into the water, and came foorth againe,
And fawnd on me, as if a man should say,
Helpe out a man that heere lyes murthered.
At first I tooke delight to see the dog,
Thinking in vaine some game did there lye hid,
Amongst the Nettles growing neere the banke:
But when no game, nor any thing appear'd,
That might produce the Spaniell to this sport,
I gan to rate and beate the harmlesse Cur,
Thinking to make him leaue to follow me,
But words, nor blowes, could mooue the dog away,
But still he plung'd, he diu'd, he barkt, he ran
Still to my side, as if it were for helpe:
I seeing this, did make the ditch be dragd,
Where then was found this body as you see,
With great amazement to the lookers on.

    3. Beholde the mightie miracles of God,
That sencelesse things should propagate their sinne,
That are more beastuall farre then beastlinesse,
Of any creature most insensible.

    2 neigh. Cease we to wonder at Gods wondrous works,
And let vs labour for to bring to light,
Those masked fiends that thus dishonor him:
This sack is new, and loe beholde his marke
Remaines vpon it, which did sell the bag,
Amongst the Salters we shall finde it out,
When, and to whom, this bloody bag was sold.

    3. Tis very likely, let no paines be spar'd,
To bring it out, if it be possible,
Twere pitty such a murther should remaine
Vnpunished, mongst Turkes and Infidels.

    1 neigh. Sirs, I do know the man that solde this bag,
And if you please, Ile fetch him presently.

    Gent. With all our harts, how say you Gentlemen?

Per-

Perchance the murther thus may come to light.

    3. I pray you do it, we will tarry heere: *Exut.1.neigh.*
And let the eyes of euery paſſenger
Be ſatiſſied, which may example be,
How they commit ſo dreadfull wickedneſſe.

   Ent. wom. And pleaſe your maiſterſhips the boy is dead.

   3.neigh. Tis very ſtrange, that hauing many wounds,
So terrible, ſo ghaſtlie, which is more,
Hauing the hammer ſticking in his head,
That he ſhould liue and ſtirre from Friday night,
To Sunday morning, and euen then depart,
When that his Maiſters mangled courſe were found,
Bring him foorth too, perchance the murtherers
May haue their hearts touched with due remorſe,
Viewing their deeds of damned wickedneſſe.

      Bring forth the boye and lay him by Beech.

   1.neigh. Here is the Salters man that ſolde the bag,

   Gent. My friend, how long ſince did you ſell that bag?
And vnto whom, if you remember it?

   Sal. I ſould the bag good ſir but yeſterday,
Vnto a maide, I do not know her name.

   3.neigh. Nor where ſhe dwels.   *Sal.* No certeinly.

   2.neigh. But what apparell had ſhe on her back?

   Sal. I do not well remember what ſhe wore,
But if I ſaw her I ſhould know her ſure.

   3 neigh. Go round about to euery neighbors houſe,
And will them ſhew their maides immediatly:
God graunt we may finde out the murtherers.

      Go to one houſe, and knock at doore, asking,
Bring forth ſuch maides as are within your houſe.

   1.houſekeeper. I haue but one, ile ſend her downe to you.

   3.neigh. Is this the maide.   *Come out maide.*

   Salt. No ſir, this is not ſhe.   *Go to another, &c.*
How many maides do dwell within this houſe?

   2.houſe. Her's nere a woman here, except my wiſe.

      Go to Merryes.

   3.neigh. Whoſe houſe is this?

Lon. An honeſt ciuill mans,cald *Maiſter Merry,*
Who I dare be ſworne,would neuer do ſo great a murther
But you may aske heere to for faſhion ſake.

    Rachel *ſits in the ſhop.*

 3. How now faire maide,dwels any here but you?
Thou haſt too true a face for ſuch a deed.

 Rach. No gentle ſir,m y brother keepes no more.

 3.neigh This is not ſhe? *Sal.* No tiu'ly gentlemã.*Ex.R.*

 3. This will not ſerue,we cannot finde her out ,
Bring in thoſe bodyes,it growes towards night,
God bring theſe damn d murtherers at length to light.

         Exeunt omnes.

    Enter Merry *and* Rachel,

 Mer, Why go the neighbours round abont the ſtreete
To euery houſe ? what haſt thou heard the cauſe ?

 Rach They go about with that ſame Salters man,
Of whom I bought the bag but yeſterday,
To ſee if he can know the maide againe
Which bought it,this I thinke the very cauſe.

 Mer, How were my ſences ouercome with feare,
That I could not foreſee this ieopardy :
For had I brought the bag away with me,
They had not had this meanes to finde it out.
Hide thee aboue leaſt that the Salters man,
Take notice of thee that thou art the maide,
And by that knowledge we be all vndone.

 Rach That feare is paſt,I ſawe,I ſpake with him,
Yet he denies that I did buy the bag :
Beſides,the neighbors haue no doubt of you,
Saying you are an honeſt harmeleſſe man,
And made enquirie heere for faſhion ſake.

 Mer. My former life,deſerues their good conceits,
Were it not blemiſht with this treacherie.
My heart is merier then it was before,
For now I hope the greateſt feare is paſt,
The hammer is denyed,the bag vnknowne,
Now there is left no meanes to bring it out,

           Vnleſſe

Vnlesse our selues prooue Traitors to our selues.

Rach. When saw you *Harry Williams*? *Me* Why to day
I met him comming home from *Powles* Cresse,
Where he had beene to heare a Sermon.

Rach Why brought you not the man along with you
To come to dinner, that we might perswade
Him to continue in his secrecie.

Mer. I did intreate him, but he would not come,
But vow'd to be as secret as my selfe.

Rach. What, did he sweare?

Mer. What neede you aske me that?
You know we neuer heard him sweare an othe.
But since he hath conceal'd the thing thus long,
I hope in God he will conceale it still.

Rach Pray God he do, and then I haue no doubt,
But God will ouerpasse this greeuous sinne,
If you lament with true vnfained teares,
And seeke to liue the remnant of your yeares,
In Gods true feare with vpright conscience.

Mer. If it would please him pardon this amisse,
And rid my body from the open shame,
That doth attend this deed, being brought to light,
I would endeuour all my comming dayes,
To please my maker, and exalt his praise.
But it growes late, come bring me to my bed,
That I may rest my sorrow charged head.

Rach. Rest still in calme secure tranquillitie,
And ouer-blowe this storme of nightie feare,
With pleasant gales of hoped quietnesse,
Go when you will, I will attend, and pray,
To send this wofull night a cheerefull day.   *Exeunt.*

Enter Falleria *and* Softrata
weeping.

Fall. Passe ore these rugged furrowes of laments,
And come to plainer pathes of cheerefulnesse,
Cease thy continuall showers of thy woe,

And

And let my pleasing wordes of comfort chase,
This duskie cloudes of thy vniust dispaire,
Farre from thy hart, and let a pleasing hope,
Of young Pertillos happy safe returne,
Establish all your ill deuining thoughts,
So shall you make me cheerefull that am sad,
And feede your hopes with fond illusions.

   Sof. I could be so, but my diuided soule,
Twixt feare and hope of young Pertillos life,
Cannot ariue at the desired port,
Of firme beleefe, vntill mine eyes do see,
Him that I sent to know the certaineue.

   Fal. To know the certaintie, of whom, of what,
Whome, whether, when, or where about I praie,
Haue you dispatcht a frustrate messenger,
By heauen, and earth, my heart misguiseth me,
They will preuent my cunning pollicie.   *To the people.*
Why speake you not what winged *Pegasus*,
Is posted for your satisfaction.

   Sof. Me thinkes my speach reueales a hidden feare,
And that feare telles me, that the childe is dead.

   Fall. By sweete S. *Andrew* and my fathers soule,
I thinke the peeuish boy be too too well:
But speake, who was your passions harbinger.

   Sof. One that did kindle my misdoubting thoughts,
With the large flame of his timiddity.

   Fall. Oh then I know the tinder of your feare,
Was young *Allenso* your white honnie sonne:
Confusion light vpon his timerous head,
For broching this large streame of feare fulnesse,
And all the plagues that damned furies feele,
For their forepassed bold iniquities:
Afflict you both for thus preuenting me.

   Sof Preuenting you, of what, *Fallerto* speake,
For if you doe not, my poore hart will breake.

   Fall. Why of the good that I had purposed,
To young *Pertillo*, which I would conceale,

From

From you, and him, vntill the deed were done.

    Soft. If it were good, then we affect him deare,
And would adde furtherance to your enterprise.

    Fall. I say your close ease-dropping policies,
Haue hindred him of greater benefits,
Then I can euer do him after this :
If he liue long, and growe to riper sinne,   *To the people*
Heele curse you both, that thus haue hindered
His freedome from this goale of sinfull flesh :
But let that passe, when went your harebrainde sonne,
That Cuckow vertue-singing, hatefull byrde,
To guarde the safetie of his better part,
Which he hath pend within the childish coope,
Of young *Pertillos* sweete securitie.

    Soft. That louely sonne, that comfort of my life,
That roote of vertuous magnamitie,
That doth affect with an vnfained loue,
That tendet boy, which vnder heauens bright eye,
Deserueth most to be affected deare,
Went some two houres after the little boy
Was sent away, to keepe at *Padua*.

    Fall. What is a louelie ? he's a loathsome toade,
A one eyde *Cyclops*, a stigmaticke brat,
That durst attempt to contradict my will,
And prie into my close intendements.

        Enter Alenso *sad*.
Mas here a comes, his downcast sullen looke,
Is ouer waigh'd with mightie discontent,
I hope the brat is posted to his sire,
That he is growne so lazie of his pace :
Forgetfull of his dutie, and his tongue,
Is euen fast tyde with strings of heauinesse.
Come hether boye, sawst thou my obstacle,
That little *Dromus* that crept into my sonne,
With friendly hand, remoou'd and thrust away,
Say I, and please me with the sweetest note,
That euer relisht in a mortals mouth.

        H   *Alen.*

To haue such power in my death bringing voice,
See how in steade of teares and hartie sighes:
Of foulded armes and sorrow speaking lookes,
I doe behold with cheere full countenance,
The liuelesse roote of my natiuitie:
And thanke her hasty soule that thence did goe,
To keepe her from her sonne and husbandes woe.
Now father giue attention to my tale:
I will not dip my griefe deciphering tongue,
In bitter woides of reprehension,
Your deeds haue throwne more mischiefes on your head
Then wit or reason can remoue againe;
For to be briefe, *Pertillo*, oh that name
Cannot be nam'de without a hearty sigh,
Is murthered, and,   *Fal.* What and, this newes is good.
    Allen. The men which you suborn'd to murther him.
    Fal. Better and better, then it cannot out,
Vnlesse your loue will be so scripulous,
That it will ouerthrowe your selfe and me.
    Allen. The best is last, and yet you hinder me,
The Duke of *Padua* hunting in the wood:
Accompanied with Lordes and gentlemen,
    Fal. Swones what of that? what good can come of that?
    Allen. Was made acquainted by the one of them,
(That had some little remnant of his life:)
With all your practice and conspiracie?
    Fall. I would that remnant had fled quicke to hell,
To fetch fierce findes to rend their carcases,
Rather then bring my life in ieopardie:
Is this the best, swones doe you mocke me sonne,
And make a iest at my calamitie.
    Allen. Not I good father, I will ease your woe,
If you but yeeld vnto my pollicie.
    Fal. Declare it then, my wits are now to seeke,
That peece of life hath so confounded mee,
That I am wholly ouercome with feare.
    Allen. The duke hath vow'd to prosecute your life,

With

With all the strict seueritie he can,
But I will crosse his resolution:
And keepe you from his furie well enough,
Ile weare your habit, I will seeme the man,
That did suborne the bloodie murtherers,
I will not stir from out this house of woe,
But waight the comming of the officers,
And answere for you fore the angrie Duke,
And if neede be suffer your punishment.

   Fall. Ile none of that, I do not like the last,
I loue thee dearer then I doe my life,
And all I did, was to aduance thy state,
To sunne bright beames of shining happinesse.

   Allen. Doubte not my life, for when I doe appeare
Before the duke, I being not the man,
He can inflict no punishment on mee.

   Fall. Mas thou saiest true, a cannot punish thee,
Thou wert no actor of their Tragædie:
But for my beard thou canst not counterfet,
And bring gray haires vppon thy downy chinne,
White frostes are neuer seene in summers spring.

   Allen. I bought a beard this day at *Padua*,
Such as our common actors vse to weare:
When youth would put on ages countenaunce,
So like in shape, in colour, and in all,
To that which growes vpon your aged face,
That were I dressed in your abilimentes,
Your selfe would scarcely know me from your selfe.

   Fal. That's excellent, what shape hast thou deuis'd,
To be my vizard to delude the worlde:

   Allen. Why thus, ile presentlie shaue off your haire,
And dresse you in a lowlie shepheardes weede,
Then you will seeme to haue the carefull charge,
Of some wealth bringing rich and fleecy flocke,
And so passe currant from suspition.

   Fall. This care of thine my sonne doth testifie,
Nature in thee hath firme predominance,

                 That

That neither losse of friend, nor vile reproch,
Can shake thee with their strongest violence:
In this disguise,ile see the end of thee,
That thou acquited, then maist succour me.

 Allen. I am assur'd to be exempt from woe.   *People.*
This pl.. will worke my certaine ouerthrow.

 Fall. I will beare hence thy mother,and my wife,
Vntimely murthered with true sorrowes knife.   *Exit.*

 Allen. Vntimely murthered,happy was that griefe,
Which hath abridg'd whole numbers,numberlesse:
Of hart surcharging deplorations.
She shall haue due and christian funerall,
And rest in peace amongst her auncestors,
As for our bodies,they shall be inter'd,
In rauening mawes, of Rauens,Puttockes,Crowes,
Of tatlin Magpies,and deathes harbingers,
That wilbe glutted with winde shaken limmes,
Of blood delighting hatefull murtherers:
And yet these many winged sepulchers,
Shall turne to earth so I,and father shall,
At last attaine to earth by funerall,
Well I will prosecute my pollicy,
That wished death may end my miseries.   *Exit*

  Enter Cowley, *and* Williams.

 Cow. Still in your dumpes, good *Harry* yet at last,
Vtter your motiue of this heauinesse:
Why go you not vnto your maisters house?
What are you parted? if that be the cause,
I will prouide you of a better place.

 Wil. Who roues all day,at length may hit the marke,
That is the cause,because I cannot stay,
With him whose loue,is dearer then my life.

 Cow. Why fell you out? why did you part so soone?

 Wil. We fell not out, but feare hath parted vs.

 Cow. What did he feare your truth or honest life?

 Wil. No,no, your vnderstanding is but dimme,

    That

That farre remooued, cannot iudge the feare,
We both were fearefull, and we both did part,
Becaufe indeed we both were timerous.

   Cow. What accident begot your mutuall feare?

   VVil. That which my hart hath promif'd to conceale.

   Cow. Why now you fall into your auncient vaine.

   VVil Tis vaine to vrge me from this filent vaine,
I will conceale it, though it breed my paine.

   Cow. It feemie to be a thing of confequence,
And therefore prithie *Harry* for my loue,
Open this clofe faft clafped myfterie.

   VVil. Were I-affur'd my heart fhould haue releafe,
Of fecret torment, and diftemperature,
I would reueale it to you fpecially,
Whom I haue found my faithfull fauorite.

   Cow. Good *Harrie VVilliams* make no doubt of that,
Befides, your griefe reueald may haue reliefe,
Beyond your prefent expectation:
Then tell it *Harry*, what foere it be,
And eafe your hart of horror, me of doubt.

   VVil. What haue you heard of *Beech* of *Lambert* hill?
And of his boy which late were murthered.

   Cow. I heard, and fawe, their mangled carcafes.

   VVil. But haue you heard of them that murthered them?

   Cow. No, would I had, for then Ide blafe their fhame,
And make them pay due penance for their finne.

   VVil. This I mifdoubted; therefore will forbeare,
To vtter what I thought to haue reueald.

   Cow. Knowft thou the actors of this murthrous deed,
And wilt conceale it now the deed is done?
Alas poore man, thou knoweft not what thou dooft,
Thou haft incur'd the danger of the lawe,
And thou mongft them muft fuffer punifhment,
Vnleffe thou do confeffe it prefentlie.

   VVil What? fhall I then betray my maifters life?

   Cow. Better then hazard both thy life and foule,
To boulfter out fuch barbarous villanie.

                            Why

Why then belike your maiſter did the deed.

VVil. My maiſter vnawares eſcapt my mouth,
But what the Lord doth pleaſe ſhall come to light,
Cannot be hid by humaine pollicie :
His hapleſſe hand hath wrought the fatall end,
Of *Robert Beech* and *Thomas VVincheſter.*

Cow. Could he alone do both thoſe men to death?
Hadſt thou no ſhare in execution ?

VVil Nor knew not of it, till the deed was done.

Cow. If this be true, thou maiſt eſcape with life:
Confeſſe the truth vnto the officers,
And thou ſhalt finde the fauour of the lawe.

VVil. If I offended,'twas my Maiſters loue,
That made me hide his great tranſgreſſions:
But I will be directed as you pleaſe,
So ſaue me God, as I am innocent. *Exeunt.*

Enter Alenſo *in* Falleriaes *apparrell and berd,* Falleria
ſhauen to ſhepheards habillments.

Fal. Part of my ſelfe, now ſeemſt thou wholy me,
And I ſeeme neither like my ſelfe, nor thee :
Thankes to thy care, and this vnknowne diſguiſe.
I like a ſhepheard now muſt learne to know,
When to lead foorth my little bleating flock,
To pleaſing paſtures, and well fatting walkes,
In ſtormie time to driue them to the lee,
To cheere the pretie Lambes, whoſe bleating voice,
Doth craue the wiſhed comfort of their dams,
To ſound my merry Bag-pipe on the downes,
In ſhearing times poore ſhepheards feſtiuals,
And laſtlie, how to driue the Wolfe away,
That ſeeke to make the little Lambes their pray.

Allen Ah haue you care to driue the Wolfe away,
From ſillie creatures wanting intellecte,
And yet would ſuffer your deuouring thoughts,
To ſuck the blood of your dead brothers ſonne,

As

As pure and innocent as any lambe,
Pertillo was, which you haue fed vpon,
But things paſt helpe may better be bewaild
With carefull teares, then finde a remedie,
Therefore for feare our practiſe be eſpide,
Let vs to queſtion of our husbandrie,
How many Lambes fell from the middle flock,
Since I my selfe did take the latter view.

              Enter Veſunio, Turqual. Alberto.

  Fall. Some viue and twenty, whereof two are dead,
But three and twenty ſcud about the fields,
That glads my hart to ze their iollitie.

  Veſu. This is the man, conferring of his Lambes,
That ſlew a Lambe worth all his flock beſides.

  Alin. When is the time to let the Weathers blood,
The forward ſpring, that had ſuch ſtore of graſſe,
Hath fild them full of ranke vnwholſome blood,
Which muſt be purg'd, elſe when the winter comes,
The rot will leaue me nothing but their skinnes.

  Fall. Chil let om blood, but yet it is no time,
Vntill the zygne be gone below the hart.

  Veſu. Forbeare a while this idle buſineſſe,
And talke of matters of more conſequence.

  Fall. Che tell you plaine, you are no honeſt man,
To call a ſhepheards care an idle toye,
What though we haue a little merry ſport,
With flowrie gyrlonds, and an Oaten pipe,
And iolly friskins on a holly-day,
Yet is a ſhepheards cure, a greater carke,
Then ſweating Plough-men with their buſie warke.

  Veſu. Hence leaue your ſheepiſh ceremoniall,
And now *Fallerio*, in the Princes name,
I do arreſt you, for the cruell murther
Of young *Pertillo* left vnto your charge,
Which you diſcharged with a bloody writ,
Sign'd by the hands of thoſe you did ſuborne:
Nay looke not ſtrange, we haue ſuch euidence,

                            To

To ratifie your Stigian cruelty,
That cannot be deluded any way:

   Allen. Alas my Lords, I know not what you say,
As for my Nephew, he I hope is well,
I sent him yesterday to *Padua.*

   Alber. I, he is well, in such a vengers handes,
As will not winck at your iniquity.

   Allen. By heauen and earth my soule is innocent,
Say what you will, I know my conscience.

   Fal. To be afflicted with a scourge of care,
Which my oreweaning rashnesse did inflict.

   Turq. Come beare him hence, expostulate no more,
That heart that could inuent such treachery,
Can teach his face to braue it cunninglie.

   Alen. I do defie your accusations,
Let me haue iustice I will answere it.

   Vesuu. So beare him hence, I meane to stay behinde,
To take possession of his goods and landes:
For the Dukes vse, it is too manifest.

   Allen. I hope youle answere any thing you doe,
My Lord *Vesuuo* you shall answere it:
And all the rest that vse extremities.

   Alber. I to the Dukes Exchecker not to you.

                 Exeunt omnes manet Falleria.

   Fal. Thus shades are caught when substances are fled,
Indeede they haue my garments, but my selfe,
Am close enough from their discouerie,
But not so close but that my verie soule,
Is ract with tormentes for *Pertillos* death;
I am *Actern,* I doe beare about
My hornes of shame and inhumanitie,
My thoughts, like hounds which late did flatter me:
With hope of great succeeding benefits.
Now gin to teare my care-tormented heart,
With feare of death and tortring punishment,
These are the stings when as our consciences,
Are stuf'd and clogd with close concealed crimes,

           I   –   Well

Well I muſt ſmoather all theſe diſcontentes,
And ſtriue to beare a ſmoother countenaunce:
Then rugged care would willingly permit,
Ile to the Court to ſee *Allenſo* free,
That he may then relieue my pouertie.　　　　*Exit.*

　　　Enter Conſtable, three watchmen with
　　　　　　　Halberdes.

　・・*Con.* Who would haue thought of all the men aliue,
That *Thomas Merry* would haue done this deede:
So full of ruth and monſtrous wickedneſſe.
　1.wat. Of all the men that liue in London walles.
I would haue thought that *Merry* had bin free,
　2.wat. Is this the fruites of Saint-like Puritans,
I neuer like ſuch damn'd hipocriſie.
　3.wat. He would not loaſe a ſermon for a pound,
An oath he thought would rend his iawes in twaine,
An idle word did whet Gods vengeance on:
And yet two muthers were not ſcrupulous,
Such cloſe illuſions God will bring to light,
And ouerthrowe the workers with his might.
　Con. This is the houſe, come let vs knocke at dore,
I ſee a light they are not all in bed:
　　　　　　Knockes, Rachell comes downe.
How now faire maide, is your brother vp?
　Rach. He's not within ſir, would you ſpeake with him?
　Con. You doe but ieſt, I know he is within,
And I muſt needes go vppe and ſpeake with him.
　Rach. In deede good ſir, he is in bed aſleepe,
And I was loath to trouble him to night.
　Con. Well ſiſter, I am ſorry for your ſake,
But for your brother, he is knowne to be
A damned villaine and an hipocrite,
Rachell, I charge thee in her highneſſe name,
To go with vs to priſon preſently.
　Rach. To priſon ſir, alas what haue I done?
　Con. You know that beſt, but euery one doe know,
　　　　　　　　　　　　　　　　You

You and your brother murthered maister *Beech*,
And his poore boy that dwelt at Lambert hill.

   Rach. I murthered, my brother knowes that I
Did not consent to either of their deathes.

   Con. That must be tride, where doth your brother lye?

   Rach. Here in his bed, me thinks he's not a sleepe.

   Con. Now maister *Merry*, are you in a sweate.

                    Throwes his night cap away.

   Merry sigh. No verily, I am not in a sweate.

   Con. Some sodaine feare affrights you, whats the cause?

   Mer. Nothing but that you wak'd me vnawares.

   Con. In the Queenes name I doe commaund you rise,
And presently to goe along with vs.   *Riseth vp.*

   Mer. With all my hart, what doe you know the cause?

   Con. We partly doe, when saw you maister *Beech?*

   Mer. I doe not well remember who you meane.

   Con. Not *Beech* the chaundler vpon Lambert hill.

   Mer. I know the man, but saw him not this fortnight.

   Con. I would you had not, for your sisters sake,
For yours, for his, and for his harmelesse boy,
Be not obdurate in your wickednesse,
Confession drawes repentance after it.

   Mer. Well maister Constable I doe confesse,
I was the man that did them both to death:
As for my sister and my harmelesse man,
I doe protest they both are innocent.

   Con. Your man is fast in hold, and hath confest,
The manner how, and where, the deede was done:
Therefore twere vaine to colour any thing,
Bring them away.   *Rach.* Ah brother woe is me,

  Mer. I comfortlesse will helpe to comfort thee. *Exeunt.*

Enter *Trueth.*

Weepe, weepe poore soules, & enterchange your woes,
Now *Merry* change thy name and countenance:
Smile not, thou wretched creature, least in scorne,
Thou smile to thinke on thy extremities,

                            Thy

Thy woes were countlesse for thy wicked deedes,
Thy sisters death neede not increase the coumpt,
For thou couldst neuer number them before :
Gentles helpe out with this suppose I pray,
And thinke it truth for Truth dooth tell the tale.
Merry by lawe conuict, as principall,
Receiues his doome, to hang till he be dead,
And afterwards for to be hangd in chaines:
Williams and *Rachell* likewise are conuict
For their concealement, *VVilliams* craues his booke,
And so receaues a brond of infamie.
But wretched *Rachels* sexe denies that grace,
And therefore dooth receiue a doome of death,
To dye with him, whose sinnes she did conceale.
Your eyes shall witnesse of their shaded tipes,
Which many heere did see perform'd indeed:
As for *Fallerio*, not his homelie weedes,
His beardlesse face, nor counterfetted speech,
Can shield him from deserued punishment :
But what he thinkes shall rid him from suspect ,
Shall drench him in more waues of wretchednesse,
Pulling his sonne into relentlesse iawes,
Of hungrie death, on tree of infamie :
Heere comes the Duke that doomes them both to die,
Next *Merries* death shall end this Tragedie.   *Exit.*

Enter Duke, Vesuuio, Turq. Alberto :
and Fallerio *disguised.*

Duke. Where is that *Syren*, that incarnate fiend,
Monster of Nature, spectacle of shame,
Blot and confusion of his familie,
False seeming semblance of true-dealing trust,
I meane *Fallerio* bloody murtherer.
Hath he confest his cursed treacherie,
Or will he stand to prooue his innocence.
      Vesu. We haue attach'de *Fallerio* gracious Lord,
And did accuse him with *Pertillos* death :
But

But he remote, will not confesse himselfe,
Neither the meanes, nor author of the same,
His mightie vowes and protestations,
Do almost seeme to pleade integritie,
But that we all do know the contrarie.

   Fall. I know your error stricks your knowledge blinde,
His seeming me, doth so delude your minde.   *People.*

   Duke. Then bring him forth, to answer for himselfe,
Since he stands stoutly to denie the deed:

              Alberto and other fetch Alenso.

His sonne can witnesse, that the dying man,
Accusde *Fallerio* for his treacherie.
Stand forth thou close disguised hipocrite,
And speake directlie to these articles,
First, didst thou hire two bloodie murtherers
To massacre *Pertillo* in a wood?

   Alen. I neuer did suborne such murtherers,
But euer lou'd *Pertillo* as my life.

   Duke. Thy sonne can witnesse to the contrarie.

   Alen. I haue no sonne to testifie so much.

   Fab. No, for his grauitie is counterfeit,
Pluck of his beard, and you will sweare it so.

   Vesu Haue you no sonne? doth not *Alenso* liue?

   Alen. *Alenso* liues, but is no sonne of mine.

   Alber. Indeed his better part had not his source,
From thy corrupted vice affecting hart,
For vertue is the marke he aimeth at.

   Duke. I dare be sworne that *Sostrata* would blush,
Shouldst thou deny *Alenso* for thy sonne.

   Alen. Nay did she liue, she would not challenge me,
To be the father of that haplesse sonne.

   Turq. Nay, then anon you will denie your selfe,
To be your selfe, vniust *Fallerio.*

   Alen. I do confesse my selfe, to be my selfe,
But will not answere to *Fall. rio.*

   Duke. Not to *Fallerio*, this is excellent,
You are the man was cal'd *Fallerio.*

Alen. He neuer breathed yet that cal'd me so,
Except he were deceiu'd as you are now.

Duke. This impudence shall not excuse your fault,
You are well knowne to be *Fallerio,*
The wicked husband of dead *Sostrata,*
And father to the vertuous *Alenso.*
And euen as sure as all these certeinties,
Thou didst contriue thy little Nephewes death.

Al'n. True, for I am nor false *Fallerio,*
Husband, nor father, as you do suggest,
And therefore did not hire the murtherers:
Which to be true acknowledge with your eyes.
                    Puls off his disguise.

Duke. How now my Lords, this is a myracle,
To shake off thirtie yeares so sodeinlie,
And turne from feeble age to flourishing youth.

Alb. But he my Lord that wrought this miracle,
Is not of power to free himselfe from death,
Through the performance of this suddaine change.

Duke. No, were he the chiefest hope of Christendome,
He should not liue for this presumption:
Vse no excuse, *Alenso* for thy life,
My doome of death shall be irreuocable.

Alen. Ill fare his soule, that would extenuate
The rigor of your life confounding doome:
I am prepar'd with all my hart to die,
For thats th'end of humaine miserie.

Duke. Then thus, you shall be hang'd immediatly,
For your illusion of the Magistrates,
With borrowed shapes of false antiquitie.

Alen. Thrice happy sentence, which I do imbrace,
With a more feruent and vnfained zeale,
Then an ambicious rule desiring man,
Would do a Iem bedecked Diadem,
Which brings more watchfull cares and discontent,
Then pompe, or honor, can remunerate:
When I am dead, let it be said of me,
                                        Alenso

Alonso died to set his father free.

Pal. That were a freedome worse then seruitude,
To cruell Turke, or damned Infidell:
Most righteous Iudge, I do appeale for Iustice,
Iustice on him that hath deserued death,
Not on *Alenso*, he is innocent.

Alen. But I am guiltie of abbetting him,
Contrarie to his Maiesties Edict,
And therefore death is meritorious.

Fall. I am the wretch that did subborne the slaues,
To murther poore *Perillo* in the wood,
Spare, spare *Alenso*, he is innocent.

Duke. What strange appeale is this, we know thee not,
None but *Fallerio* is accusde hereof.

Alen. Then father get-you hence, depart in time,
Least being knowne you suffer for the crime.

Fal. Depart, and leaue thee clad in horrors cloake,
And suffer death for true affection:
Although my soule be guiltie of more sinne,
Then euer sinfull soule were guiltie of:
Yet fiends of hell would neuer suffer this,
I am thy father, though vnworthy so:
Oh still I see these weedes do seare your eyes:
I am *Fallerio*, make no doubt of me.   *Put off.*
Though thus disguisde, in habite, countenance,
Only to scape the terror of the lawe.

Alen. And I *Alenso* that did succour him,
Gainst your commaundement, mightie Soueraigne.
Ponder your oath, your vowe, as God did liue,
I should not liue, if I did rescue him:
I d.d, God liues, and will reuenge it home,
If you defer my condigne punishment.

Duke. Assure your selues you both shall suffer death:
But for *Fallerio*, he shall hang in chaines,
After he's dead, for he was principall.

Fall. Vnsauerie Woormewood, Hemlock, bitter gall,
Brings no such bad, vnrelisht, lower taste,

Vnto the tongue, as this death boding voice,
Brings to the eares of poore *Fallerio*.
Not for my selfe but for *Allensoes* sake,
Whome I haue murthered by my trechery:
Ah my dread Lord, if any little sparke,
Of melting pittie doth remaine aliue,
And not extinguisht by my impious deedes,
Oh kindle it vnto a happie flame,
To light *Allenso* from this miserie;
Which through dim death he's like to fall into.

   Allen. That were to ouerthrow my foule and all,
Should you reuerse this sentence of my death:
My selfe would play the death man on my selfe,
And ouertake your swift and winged soule,
Ere churlish *Caron* had transported you,
Vnto the fields of sad *Proserpina*.

   Duke. Cease, cease *Fallerio*, in thy bootlesse prayers,
I am resolu'd, I am inexorable,
Vesuuio, see their iudgement be performde,
And vse *Alenso* with all clemencie:
Prouided that the lawe be satisfied.

           Exit Duke and Alberto.

   Vesu. It shall be done with all respectiuenesse,
Haue you no doubt of that my gratious Lord.

   Fal. Here is a mercie mixt with equitie,
To shew him fauour, but cut off his head.

   Alen. My reuerend father, pacifie your selfe,
I can, and will, indure the stroake of death,
Were his appearance nere so horrible,
To meete *Pertillo* in another world.

   Fal. Thou shouldst haue tarried vntill natures course
Had beene extinct, that thou oregrowne with age,
Mightst die the death of thy progeuitors,
Twas not thy meanes he died so soddenly,
But mine, that causing his, haue murthred thee.

   Alen. But yet I slew my mother, did I not?

   Fal. I, with reporting of my villanie.

                    The

The very audit of my wickednesse,
Had force enough to giue a sodaine death:
Ah sister, sister, now I call to minde,
Thy dying wordes now prou'd a prophesie,
If you deale ill with this distressed childe:
God will no doubt reuenge the innocent,
I haue delt ill, and God hath tane reuenge.

   Allen. Now let vs leaue remembrance of past deedes,
And thinke on that which more concerneth vs.

   Fal. With all my hart thou euer wert the spur,
Which prickt me on to any godlinesse:
And now thou doest indeuor to incite,
Me make my parting peace with God and men:
I doe confesse euen from my verie soule,
My hainous sinne and grieuous wickednesse,
Against my maker manie thousand waies:
Ab imo cordis I repent my selfe,
Of all my sinnes against his maiestie:
And heauenly father lay not to my charge,
The death of poore *Pertillo* and those men,
Which I suborn'd to be his murtherers,
When I appeare before thy heauenlie throne,
To haue my sentence, or of life or death.

   Vesu. Amen, amen, and God continue still,
These mercie mouing meditations.

   Allen. And thou great God which art omnipotent,
Powerfull enough for to redeeme our soules:
Euen from the verie gates of gaping hell,
Forgiue our sinnes, and wash away our faults:
In the sweete riuer of that precious blood,
Which thy deare sonne did shed in *Galgotha*,
For the remission of all contrite soules.

   Fal. Forgiue thy death my thrice beloued sonne.
   Allen. I doe, and father pardon my misdeedes,
Of disobedience and vnthankfullnesse.

   Fal. Thou neuer yet wert disobedient,
Vnlesse I did commaund vnlawfulnesse,

K

Vn-

Vngratefulnesse did neuer trouble thee,
Thou art too bounteous thus to guerdon me.

Allen. Come let vs kisse and thus imbrace in death,
Euen when you will come bring vs to the place:
Where we may consumate our wretchednesse,
And change it for eternall hapinesse.　　　*Exeunt omnes.*

Enter Merry *and* Rachel *to execution with Offi-*
cers with Halberdes, the Hangman
with a lather, &c.

Mer. Now sister *Rachell* is the houre come,
Wherein we both must satisfie the law,
For *Beeches* death and harmelesse *Winchester:*
Weepe not sweete sister, for that cannot helpe,
I doe confesse fore all this company,
That thou wert neuer priuie to their deathes,
But onelie helpest me when the deede was done,
To wipe the blood and hide away my sinne,
And since this fault hath brought thee to this shame,
I doe intreate thee on my bended knee,
To pardon me for thus offending thee.

Rach. I doe forgiue you from my verie soule,
And thinke not that I shed these store of teares,
For that I price my life, or feare to dye,
Though I confesse the manner of my death,
Is much more grieueuous then my death it selfe;
But I lament for that it hath beene said,
I was the author of this crueltie,
And did produce you to this wicked deede,
Whereof God knowes that I am innocent.

Mer. Indeed thou art, thy conscience is at peace,　*Goe vp*
And feeles no terror for such wickednesse,　　*the lather.*
Mine hath beene vexed but is now at rest,
For that I am assur'd my hainous sinne:
Shall neuer rise in iudgement gainst my soule,
But that the blood of Iesus Christ hath power,

　　　　　　　　　　　　　　　　　　　　To

To make my purple finne as white as Snowe.
One thing good people, witneffe here with me,
That I do dye in perfect charitie,
And do forgiue, as I would be forgiuen,
Firft of my God, and then of all the world:
Ceafe publifhing that I haue beene a man,
Train'd vp in murther, or in crueltie,
For fore this time, this time is all too foone,
I neuer flue or did confent to kill,
So helpe me God as this I fpeake is true:
I could fay fomething of my innocence,
In fornication and adulterie,
But I confeffe the iufteft man aliue
That beares about the frailtie of a man,
Cannot excufe himfelfe from daily finne,
In thought, in word, and deed, fuch was my life,
I neuer hated *Beech* in all my life,
Onely defire of money which he had,
And the inciting of that foe of man,
That greedie gulfe, that great *Lauiathan*,
Did halle me on to thefe callamities,
For which, euen now my very foule dooth bleede,
God ftrengthen me with patience to endure,
This chaftifement, which I confeffe too fmall
A punifhment for this my hainous finne:
Oh be couragious fifter, fight it well,
We fhall be crown'd with immortallitie.

    Rach. I will not faint, but combat manfully,
Chrift is of power to helpe and ftrengthen me.

    Officer I pray make haft, the hower is almoft paft.

    Mer. I am prepar'd, oh God receiue my foule,
Forgiue my finnes, for they are numberleffe,
Receiue me God, for now I come to thee.

        Turne of the Lather : Rachel *fhrinketh.*
    Offi. Nay fhrinke not woman, haue a cheerefull h.t.
    Rach. I, fo I do, and yet this finfull flefh,
Will be rebellious gainft my willing fpirit.

        Come

Come let me clime thefe fteps that lead to heauen,
Although they feeme the ftaires of infamie :
Let me be merror to enfuing times,
And teach all fifters how they do conceale,
The wicked deeds, of brethren, or of friends,
I not repent me of my loue to him,
But that thereby I haue prouoked God,
To heauie wrath and indignation,
Which turne away great God, for Chriftes fake.
Ah *Harry Williams,* thou wert chiefeft caufe,
That I do drinke of this moft bitter cup,
For hadft thou opened *Beeches* death at firft,
The boy had liu'd, and thou hadft fau'd my life :
But thou art bronded with a marke of fhame,
And I forgiue thee from my very foule,
Let him and me, learne all that heare of this,
To vtter brothers or their maifters miffe,
Conceale no murther, leaft it do beget,
More bloody deeds of like deformitie.
Thus God forgiue my finnes, receiue my foule,
And though my dinner be of bitter death,
Ihope my foule fhall fup with Iefus Chrift,
And fee his prefence euerlaftingly.   *Dyeth,*

Offi. The Lord of heauen haue mercy on her foule,
And teach all other by this fpectacle,
To fhunne fuch dangers as fhe ran into,
By her mifguided taciturnitie :
Cut downe their bodies, giue hers funerall,
But let his body be conueyed hence,
To Mile-end greene, and there be hang'd in chaines.
                                Exeunt omnes.

Enter Truthe.

Tru. See here the end of lucre and defire
Of riches, gotten by vnlawfull meanes,
What monftrous euils this hath brought to paffe,
Your fcarce drie eyes giue teftimoniall,

                                                    The

The father,fonne; the fifter, brother brings,
To open fcandall, and contemptuous death.

Enter Homicide and Couetoufneffe.

But heere come they that wrought thefe deeds of ruthe,
As if they meant to plot new wickedneffe :
Whether fo faft,you damned mifcreants?
Yee vaine deluders of the credulous,
That feeke to traine men to deftruction.

Mur. Why we will on,to fet more harmes a flote,
That I may fwim in riuers of warme blood,
Out-flowing from the fides of Innocents.

Coue. I will intice the greedie minded foule,
To pull the fruite from the forbidden tree:
Yet *Tantall* like,he fhall but gluthis eye,
Nor feede his body with falubrious fruite,

Tru. Hence Stigmaticks,you fhall not harbor heare,
To practice execrable butcheries:
My felfe will bring your clofe defignes to light,
And ouerthrow your vilde confpiracies,
No hart fhall intertaine a murthrous thought,
Within the fea imbracing continent,
Where faire *Eliza* Prince of pietie,
Doth weare the peace adorned Diadem.

Coue. Mauger the worft,I will haue many harts,
That fhall affect my fecret whifperings,
The chinck of golde is fuch a pleafing crie,
That all men wifh to heare fuch harmony,
And I will place fterne murther by my fide,
That we may do more harmes then haughty pride.

Homi. Truth,now farewell,hereafter thou fhalt fee,
Ile vexe thee more with many tragedies.

Truth. The more the pitty,would the hart of man,
Were not fo open wide to entertaine,
The harmfull baites,of felfe deuouring finne,
But from the firft vnto the latter times,
It hath and will be fo eternally,
Now it remaines to haue your good aduice,

Vnto a motion of some consequence,
There is a Barke thats newly rigd for sea,
Vnmand, vnfurnishd with munition :
She must incounter with a greater foe,
Then great *Alcydes* slue in *Lerna* Lake,
Would you be pleasd to man this willing barke,
With good conceits of her intencion,
To store her with the thundring furniture,
Of smoothest smiles, and pleasing plaudiats,
She shall be able to endure the shock,
Of snarling *Zoylus*, and his cursed crue,
That seekes to sincke her in reproches waues,
And may perchance obteine a victorie,
Gainst curious carpes, and fawning Parasites :
But if you suffer her for want of ayde,
To be orewhelmd by her insulting foes,
Oh then she sinckes, that meant to passe the flood,
With stronger force to do her countrie good :
It resteth thus whether she liue or dye :
She is your Beades-man euerlastinglie.

FINIS. Rob. *Yarington.*

Laus Deo.

CPSIA information can be obtained
at www.ICGtesting.com
Printed in the USA
LVHW08s1520070918
589477LV00013B/250/P